SOFT AS BONES

Praise for *Soft as Bones*

"Chyana Marie Sage writes with an unflinching emotional clarity, lyrical prose, and a wisdom well beyond her years. Her memoir is emotionally engaging, full of light, rage, love, and pain. This book establishes Chyana as one of the strongest young voices to emerge from Canada and our nations, unafraid to speak the truths that need to be heard."

—Tanya Talaga, author of *The Knowing*

"This is a searing, poetic memoir filled with resilience and strength. Chyana Marie Sage lays bare the wounds of generational trauma with fearless honesty, and yet, within this raw and unflinching story, there is profound beauty. This book is a testament to not only Sage's strength but also to the power of Indigenous teachings, ceremony, and story for those looking to heal from long-standing suffering. A stunning, necessary read for anyone on a journey of reconciling the pain of the past with the hopes for the next generations."

—Dallas Goldtooth, writer, actor, and community organizer

"Full of rain, dew, thunderstorms, evaporation, condensation, joining waters and drying in warmth, *Soft as Bones* moves like a river across vast territories of recovery and reckoning: it moves powerfully, and runs deep, with prose that carries many worlds on its shoulders. This book does not abandon the wounded or their wounds; it does not vilify the wounders. At the core of it all is the singular and utterly compelling voice of Chyana Marie Sage: a poet, a sister, a daughter, a Cree, Métis, and Salish storyteller who has forged a language from pain, love, history, tradition, and her many worlds, from the acreage to the Ivory Tower, to tell a story of reckoning with the ways violence, caregiving, and vitality move across generations. Sage explores what it means to build a self that does not turn away from the past but is not paralyzed by it. She is a truth-teller, and she has given us an incredible gift."

—Leslie Jamison, author of *Splinters*

"Chyana Marie Sage's writing is a gift that gleams with all of its teeth and skin and soft parts of the earth. This multigenerational memoir maps survival, family, and cycles of violence that may be familiar to Indigenous communities, but here is a story that only she can tell. 'It happened here,' she marks in shattering prose—but her storytelling urges us to tend to our wounds, so that by illuminating the darkest parts of our histories we may emerge stronger than how we entered. A stunning new voice that pushes the boundaries of form, whose stories swirl across time like sweetgrass braids, like tendrils of smoke."

—Kinsale Drake, author of *The Sky Was Once a Dark Blanket*

"Gritty yet lyrical ... *Soft as Bones* is a startling, powerful memoir about surviving family trauma and First Nations perseverance."

—*Foreword*, STARRED review

"[Sage] toggles effortlessly between the roles of diarist, poet, and journalist, linking her personal history to a pattern of intergenerational violence, all without snuffing out hope for healing. Readers will be as inspired as they are horrified."

—*Publishers Weekly*

"Wisely, Sage takes us with her on a path of understanding the legacy she has inherited—before making space for her own future."

—*Literary Hub*

"Essential reading."

—*Winnipeg Free Press*

SOFT AS BONES

A MEMOIR

CHYANA MARIE SAGE

ANANSI

Published in Canada and the USA in 2025 by House of Anansi Press Inc.
houseofanansi.com

House of Anansi Press is committed to protecting our natural environment. This book is made of material from well-managed FSC®-certified forests, recycled materials, and other controlled sources.

House of Anansi Press is an eBound Digital Certified Accessible publisher. The e-book version of this book meets stringent accessibility standards and is available to readers with print disabilities.

30 29 28 27 26   2 3 4 5 6

Library and Archives Canada Cataloguing in Publication

Title: Soft as bones : a memoir / Chyana Marie Sage.
Names: Sage, Chyana Marie, author.
Identifiers: Canadiana (print) 20250117029 | Canadiana (ebook) 2025012582X | ISBN 9781487013028 (softcover) | ISBN 9781487013035 (EPUB)
Subjects: LCSH: Sage, Chyana Marie. | LCSH: Sage, Chyana Marie—Family. | LCSH: Cree women—Canada—Biography. | LCSH: Métis women—Biography. | LCSH: Generational trauma. | LCGFT: Autobiographies.
Classification: LCC E99.C88 S24 2025 | DDC 305.48/897323071—dc23

Cover design: Greg Tabor
Cover image: Piemags / Superstock
Book design and typesetting: Alysia Shewchuk

House of Anansi Press is grateful for the privilege to work on and create from the Traditional Territory of many Nations, including the Anishinabeg, the Wendat, and the Haudenosaunee, as well as the Treaty Lands of the Mississaugas of the Credit.

Canada Council for the Arts   Conseil des Arts du Canada
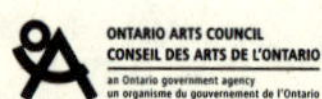

CERTIFIED CANADIAN PUBLISHER

With the participation of the Government of Canada
Avec la participation du gouvernement du Canada | Canada

We acknowledge for their financial support of our publishing program the Canada Council for the Arts, the Ontario Arts Council, and the Government of Canada.

Printed and bound in Canada

For Naia, Mckinley, Onyx, and Madden—
whose lives come from those who survived.

And for all the Native children who didn't
make it home—I wrote this for you.

♥

Some people say history moves in a spiral, not the line we have come to expect. We travel through time in a circular trajectory, our distance increasing from an epicenter only to return again, one circle removed.

—Ocean Vuong

Contents

Family Tree

Kokum Chickadee (Alice)
Robert
Kokum Thelma Chalifoux
Glen
Orleane
Darcy
Leslie
Frank
Orleane
Chyana
Chayla
Naia
Onyx
Mckinley
Madden

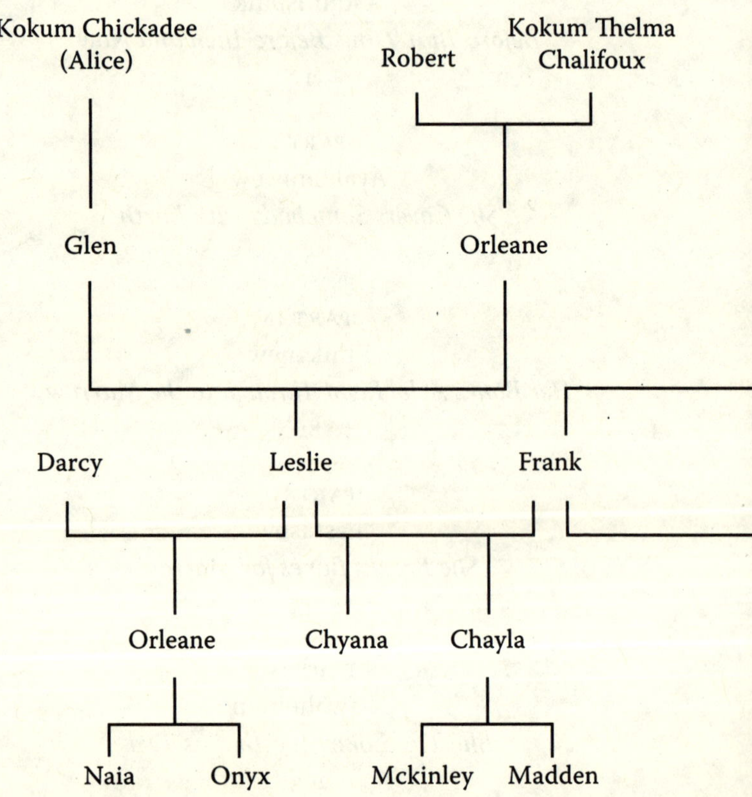

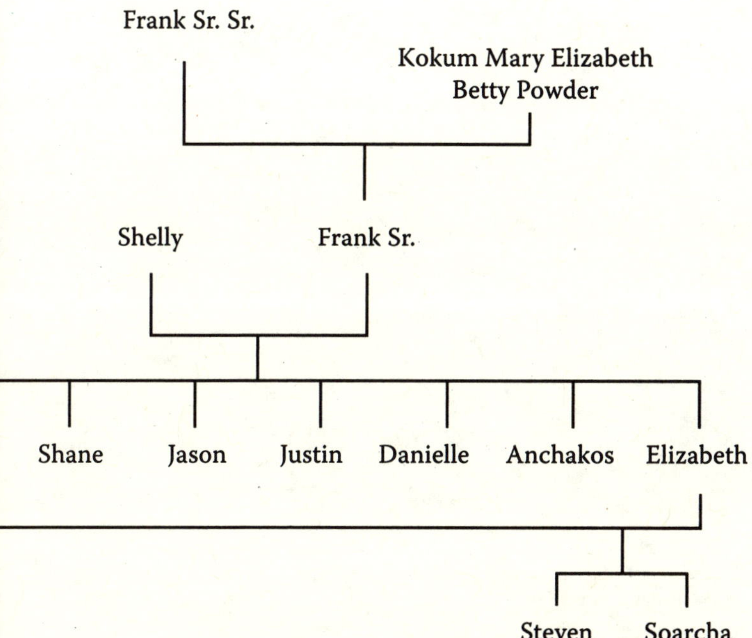
Frank Sr. Sr.
Kokum Mary Elizabeth
Betty Powder
Shelly
Frank Sr.
Shane
Jason
Justin
Danielle
Anchakos
Elizabeth
Steven
Soarcha

Astamispihk

Before That Time, Before Then and Now

I've thought over and over about the entry point to this story—our story of truth, or rather, the way that a truth can be crafted. But when the truth is crafted around a lie, the unravelling of that lie leaves a perception where reality feels precarious.

I have to unravel my father's truth, or rather, his lie, to render my reality, our reality, an honest one. We are an access point into a history—the grave consequence of schools and scoops for the Indigenous people of Turtle Island.

I write this story for all of us.

I am trying to hear a history. I am trying to hear the rapids of the river that flow past someplace beyond the bush. I am trying to hear voices of children who were buried and forgotten. I am trying to bellow their voices beyond the threat of metre sticks smacking hard against wooden desks lined with little brown fingers, and I want them to rise up as songs that reach the eagles who will carry them into the spirit realm. I am trying to hear myself as a survivor of deaths and shout from the mountaintops that every one of our deaths matters. I am trying to hear a quieting of shouts and gunshots and quiet sobs behind closed bedroom doors and my own silence.

I am trying to hear my voice—my voice, the one that could have spoken up louder and prevented so much of what I had to see. What I saw. Which could never compare to what she had to experience. She. The person I chased throughout the house—the person who put a curling iron to my hair and used barrettes to tuck the curls out of my face. Her. The one I shared a bed with for most of my life.

I am trying to hear the smallest of the three of us as she bangs on our door in a smoke-filled room and I want her to know that I always thought I locked the door to shield her, but I didn't realize that in doing so I silenced her, and I want to hear her sobs and livid laments and the sound of a phone being whipped at my forehead. I am trying to hear my apologies after I backhanded her onto the couch with my nose dripping white and I am sorry for shutting her out.

I am trying to listen to how we survived it all.

I thought I would weave our story together as three strands of thread, the way we braid sweetgrass: body, mind, spirit. But I came to realize that each strand absorbs the entirety of the others.

It is not just body.

It is not just mind.

It is not just spirit.

We are all made from the same sinew and, in fact, we are not separate at all, but so microscopically connected that lines of demarcation are almost undetectable, and you can follow the paths backward and backward and backward, never fully reaching the beginning, but rather, observing a different stage of the journey.

I could begin with my father, but I am still waiting for the gaps in his story to be filled. I could go back further and begin with Nimosôm, my grandfather, but that feels like a generation too far, even when the reverberations are still felt. I could begin with me, my beginning, because in a way that is the end, and what better way to access a history than through the end point? A tracing back with a magnifying glass as the tool.

A detective.

A grave robber.

A gravedigger, rather, laying the groundwork where all the soft bones will rest.

Part I

Ayahciniwew

She Covers Somebody with Earth

ĂKOOSIPĀYOW means it is dew, there is dew, and what is dew if not something that emerges as a result of intense pressure? It is tiny drops of water that form on cool surfaces at night. When atmospheric vapour condenses at a rate far exceeding evaporation, it leaves its mark—a residue, an imprint of the thing that came before.

I used to tell people that my father was dead. That truth was far more digestible, far less tragic, and much more acceptable for people to grasp than my truth. I was twelve years old when I buried my father alive. I don't mean that in the literal sense, but sometimes it feels like I do.

I imagined him as a burial ground, a forgotten one.

A covered-up one.

Abandoned.

One where someone would have to point out the site and declare, "It happened here. If you start digging, you will find the children."

I dreaded dinners at friends' or lovers' houses because of the inevitable question: "What do your parents do for a living?"

It's not exactly polite dinner conversation to say, "My father was a big-time crack dealer for most of my life, and now he exists someplace in British Columbia where he has two children with a girl who is the same age as me."

For someone who despises lies, this was one I granted myself. I learned from a young age that truth is something that can be crafted, and it is often tailored and specially designed to portray an image that a person wants others to see.

Everything I bring forward here is what came before the moment that shifted the rest of my life—the juncture that unravelled the beginning and reshaped the ending. I have extracted it all from memory, artifacts, journals, and now I place it in a cheesecloth, carefully balanced above the specific beakers to examine it in the way it needs to be examined. But in the end, I have a feeling that it all belongs in the same place.

I give you me—in fragments.

But how do I give you little Chy-Chy without my father? He took up so much of my space when I was a young girl. Even in his absence, he took up space. He and I were innately connected.

In some ways, we still are.

In some ways, we always will be.

There is a lot I can't remember, but the memories I do have are limited to spaces I occupied, things I was intrinsically linked to, scenes of my childhood as opposed to full stories—a bowl of soup filled with more crackers than liquid, a friend's father screaming at me, the sun shining and me, eating on a porch, food cooked in the Easy-Bake Oven gifted to me by the first boy I had a crush on, who was a foster kid to my dad's parents. He was blond and blue-eyed, both things I wasn't, yet both of us were akin to abandonment, not quite known to us then, but still present.

Perhaps memories are always tied to places, objects, and people because what are we, who are we, without the external forces that mould us? Who are we without what we are linked to? We are the culmination of everything that interacts with us, everything we interact with, everything that came before, and somehow all of those coalesce to shape a human being. There is external inheritance, and then there is internal, latent. The bits that make up our being on a cellular level.

When I think of those bits I recall things my mother tells me—how I was born a vivacious little girl who never liked to sit still, climbing trees all day long, catching frogs, writing songs, and running through the yard on bare feet as if pine needles didn't exist. She says I always aimed big, was fearless on the playground, a warrior for justice, and I could watch someone do something once and immediately pick it up, as if I had been born with a kind of knowing. She tells me all the ways all three of her girls were born with such different personalities, such varying core characteristics, and these, for me, are the varying shades of each soul.

MANY MOONS AGO, deep in the woodlands of Northern Alberta, lived evil spirits known as Witigos. They had hearts made of ice, and appetites that could only be satisfied by the blood and flesh of human beings. As dark entities, Witigos were drawn to inhabit bodies with souls that had lowered their vibrations, as this made them easier to pry into. There are many factors that weaken a soul: alcohol, drugs, depression, anxiety, abuse, exerting control over another being, mistreating people, mistreating animals, mistreating the land.

On my father's side of the family, we are primarily Woodland Cree, even though we also have Saulteaux and Mohawk ancestry. Woodland Cree are deeply spiritual beings who lived day to day within, around, and through the forests: hunting, trapping, following the buffalo. And because of the harsh conditions and precarious nature of survival, some of the most powerful sorcerers were Woodland Cree. They made amulets, called upon spirits to watch over and bless the hunts with offerings, and performed sacred killings—these practices were of utmost sanctity for the Woodland Cree. These sorcerers were believed to have supernatural abilities that could cause something as simple as making a person fall in love, or as deep as ensuring the death of an enemy, no matter how great the opponent's strength.

On my mother's side, we are primarily Plains Cree, who were notorious for their strength. Plains Cree showed a ruthlessness for attacking and slaughtering their enemies in the night, but even they feared the Woodland Cree for their uncanny magical abilities. But despite all the powers the Plains and Woodland Cree cumulatively possessed, they both feared deeply the Witigos and the Pakakos.

The Pakakos is a skeleton spectre who soars above the forest, preying on poor, disrespectful hunters who kill unnecessarily—those who harm an animal and let it escape, wounded and unable to defend itself against other attackers.

But the most feared of all evil spirits is the Witigo, who has the ability to possess the body of a human being and turn him into a cannibal.

The only way to eradicate that evil spirit is for the person's own family to kill him, creating cycles of harm.

Or, perhaps, that death is exactly what the family needs to stop the cycle.

KIMOWANIHTÂW is when she makes it rain, and this makes me think of a girl in a field adorned in her feathers and traditional dress, summoning the spirits of the gods to rain down and cleanse the earth alongside her. The rain dance is a way to cleanse evil spirits, releasing the people and the land from the power they hold. This idea has always resonated deep in my bones.

The most prominent space of my childhood was an acreage with vast fields, and I danced through them, rain beating down upon my head.

It was my favourite space, but before it we lived in Port Coquitlam, British Columbia, in a large white house with multiple levels. My dad, my mom, my older sister Orleane, my baby sister Chayla, and I all lived with my dad's parents and their foster kids. Nimosôm, my grandfather, was a big Cree man, and my grandmother made the best bannock around. For a long time I thought that she was Métis, but I learned that she was actually English. Nohkôm Betty Powder had said that if her son was going to marry a white woman, then she sure as hell better know how to make bannock, moccasins, and mukluks. Before she passed away, Kokum Betty taught my grandmother to become a master beader and adopt all the Woodland Cree ways.

Once, as a little girl, I woke up with a perfect braid in my hair—not a strand out of place. My mom asked my dad if he had done it while I slept, but he hadn't. I remember stroking my hair and listening to them speak about who had braided it. Nohkôm had passed away not long before this, and we determined it must have been her spirit. I was Kokum Betty's first great-grandbaby from her first grandchild: my father. Frank. A big Cree man with the same gap between his two front teeth as his father. Nimosôm.

Us Crees, we believe in spirits, visions, and dreams. We believe that each living thing possesses a spirit, which is eternal, and when we die, that spirit continues its journey in the universe.

When I was three I had a stuffed animal I loved too much. It was a black-and-white cat that I needed above all else and carried with me wherever I went. My first memory is of climbing up to the top floor of the white house, opening the window, staring down at the grass, and holding this cat in my small hands as I dangled it out of the frame. Despite feeling a pain inside my chest, I opened my fingers and watched it fall down down down until it hit the green blades below.

Momentarily, I was free. But just as quickly, I felt a sharp pain in my stomach. I ran downstairs and out the back door as quickly as I could, barefoot on the grass. I picked up the cat, hugged it in my arms, apologized, and took it inside with me.

This memory has followed me, year after year, and to this day, it is clear in my mind. As clear as a first memory can be. It's more the emotion that I call upon. A feeling of not wanting to depend on this thing, this stuffed cat I adored with all my heart, and yet, upon release, I was not ready to let it go. I needed to embrace it once again until the true moment would arise when our time together could come to an end.

I believe that our first memories are indicative of the core lesson we are meant to learn in this world, this lifetime. This stuffed cat was the precursor to the lesson I would have to learn again and again: the one of letting go.

OWISTOW means it is damp, and I think of speckled dew dotting summertime skin. When we moved to Edmonton, it felt like my skin was speckled with dew—uncomfortable. All I wanted was to run back to the coastal mountains of BC, where I could dive headfirst into the saltwater womb, swimming with the spirits of the salt.

We lived in a tiny white rental house with concrete steps leading up to the small front door, nestled between a duplex on the left, where each half was larger than our entire home, and a large pink home on the right that was three times the size of ours. Our lawn was half dirt, half dandelions and surrounded by a chain-link fence. My sisters and I used to walk to the store on the corner and buy pizza pops and jumbo freezies for a dollar.

I went to Calder School for part of kindergarten, and from this school, I have four memories.

One: No one wanted to play with me at recess because I was the new kid.

Two: The teacher called my parents because I refused to eat what they were serving for lunch—onion soup made from the cheap soup packets that most people use to make onion dip. I watched all my classmates run outside when the bell rang, and the teacher sat me at my desk, trying to force me to eat. My parents came and took one look at the meal and said they couldn't possibly expect me to eat whatever that was. I was released and ran straight for the swing set, pushing myself forward and backward, deeply.

Three: One half of the classroom was for kindergarteners, and the other half was for preschoolers. A small childproof gate separated the two. I would sit on the kindergarten side and a young blond boy would come over and sit on the other side. I would reach my small hand through one of the holes in the gate and pull his hair, quietly, so no one would notice. Perhaps there was something in his clean, white, blond face that I wanted to harm. He would come back to the gate each day, compelled toward this small brown child with dirty, bruised kneecaps reaching toward him with sticky fingers.

Four: I was with my big sister, Orleane, in the playground. We drifted down the slide and at the bottom we found a small pile of needles. We ran home, since our house was across the street, to tell our mom that we had found something that looked dangerous.

KUSKOWUNUSK is a dark cloud that holds the threat of a great rain that only the cumulonimbus can contain, and when we moved to my favourite home—the acreage—the cumulonimbus gathered, and to me it was beautiful to watch the great storms from our big bay window in the trailer and feel the walls rattle with the thunder and watch the sky light up outside while the lights went out inside—how special was the moment when my mother lit the candles, creating our hearth. But while I marvelled at the awe of it, my mother felt the weight of it.

The most formative years of my childhood were spent on the acreage, attending Camilla School. We lived there from when I was in kindergarten until grade three. Our trailer belonged to Kokum Thelma, and she rented it out to different family members over the years. My memories of this place are linked to driving toward it, approaching and anxiously awaiting the croaks of frogs, the crackling of grasshoppers, and the silence of sirens.

Driving north on the St. Albert Trail from Edmonton there was nothing to see but vast fields filled with canola, wheat, horses, and cows that framed a land of living skies that melted into everlasting sunsets fading behind Douglas, balsam, and subalpine firs. My anticipation reached its crescendo when we turned left at the main intersection that would take us to Morinville if we turned right. We had to drive slowly on the dirt and gravel road that formed small hills, up and down, for about eight kilometres until I saw the evergreen forest on the left, gently swaying in the wind, surrounding our property. Turning into the driveway, I saw the trailer up ahead and slightly to the right. On the left were tombstones for the pet cemetery.

Over the years, I buried my lovebird, Lucky; my first dog, Buddy; and Pretty Girl, the wandering cat who would disappear for months, even years, at a time before coming home, new battle wounds matted into her fur. One time she came back with half her ear missing, but she always came back, evading coyotes, cougars, and foxes.

After we parked the car, Orleane, Chayla, and I ran toward the firepit in the right front corner of the property and onto the small trail behind it that led to our secret clubhouse—a small clearing among the firs. My whole family—cousins, uncles, aunties—and all our friends would sit around that firepit, roasting hot dogs and marshmallows, making s'mores, speculating about the life that Pretty Girl must have been living. We imagined her battling predators, evading death, and then gripping mice, squirrels, and birds beneath her claws, surviving in the bush all by herself.

She eventually died peacefully under the trees in our yard.

We settled into our new home as if we had always been there, the blood memory of the prairies coursing through our veins. Each morning I ran outside to the firepit after wolfing down a bowl of Oatmeal Crisp, ready to begin my day of adventures, sisters in tow, long hair in braids breezing behind me. I was a feral little girl who delighted in bare feet covered in dirt and a T-shirt stained with sap. My mother chased me around the yard, trying to force shoes onto my feet so she wouldn't have to pick the pine needles out of them later. On my way, I often saw the snares were full. I'd yell back to the trailer, "Dad, you caught a rabbit!" before running past the carcasses and into the trees.

We gathered sticks and formed miniature teepees, popped the fuzzies off the pussy willows and placed them beside, pretending they were small animals. We snuck over onto the neighbours' property and explored their forests and old abandoned barns. We climbed all over giant wooden farming spools, and Chayla and I would squeal at the spiders while Orleane picked them up and let them crawl over her arms.

We gathered small tokens on our adventures—wooden spools, interesting sticks, small blankets of moss, special leaves, and unique pinecones—before carrying them back to our own property, where we constructed ladybug fortresses, convinced we had built them the best home there ever was. We would capture dozens and place them inside just to watch them fly away, uninterested in the life we had given them.

I lay on the dirt and watched the ants crawl over my skin, wondering how far they had travelled. Shaking off the ants, I picked out a tree and began to climb. In my pocket I kept colourful thumbtacks, and when I climbed as high as my courage allowed, I stuck a tack into the bark, knowing that the next time I climbed that tree, I would place the tack higher than before. The swaying of the tree, as I neared the top, enchanted my small limbs.

When the sun began to set and the noises of the forest whistled a warning, we burst out of the woods and ran toward the back of our trailer, past the well in the centre of the yard. We stopped when we got to the birch trees at the back, pulled off the papery bark, and practised our letters, Chayla still too small to scratch out anything legible but happy to pull off perfect little sheets.

In the farming fields behind the birches, crops grew far above our heads and we ran through them until we reached the pond. Many rocks surrounded the glistening water and we squatted low in our rubber boots and flowy shorts with mismatched shirts, watching the tadpoles transform under the surface.

My sisters dared me to run through it, and I did.

The water splashed up high around my stomping footsteps, revealing the pond floor to me at lightning speed. We saw a strange creature that didn't look like anything from this world. To this day we swear it was a teeny tiny alien. My sisters helped me hunt for it the way we hunted frogs, but we never found the mystery alien again. We lay on the big rocks surrounding the pond, our voices one with the grasshoppers and toads. When we saw the combines driving down the fields, we knew it was time to go home. We darted through the tall crops as quick as dragonflies, each second the combines inching closer and threatening our lives, until we reached the fence and climbed over—*safe*, in our yard.

We loved catching frogs. It became a game to see how many we could each catch. We always played catch and release. We poked holes in the lids of the massive old margarine containers my mother kept for us to reuse and filled them with pond water, putting our frogs inside until our competition was over. One morning, I caught twenty small tree frogs. After we tallied up our catchings, my mom called to us from the trailer. "Girls, I'm heading into town! Grab your things and come with me."

My sisters had released their frogs, but I wasn't quite ready to let mine go. I wanted to build them a sanctuary and watch them hop through it. So I put the lid on my frogs' den and placed it under a tree in the shade.

By the time we got home, the sun had moved and my margarine container was sitting in the glaring heat of the prairie summer. I took off the lid, Orleane at my side, and saw that all the frogs were belly up.

I had boiled all my frog friends alive.

I was six years old, Chayla was three, and Orleane was nine. My mother educated us about the way the earth moves throughout the day, the changing the position of the sun. We had a funeral in the pet cemetery and I never put frogs in margarine containers again.

Once a week we grabbed our wagon, filled it with wildflowers, tall grasses, carrots, celery, and occasionally apples, and set out for the neighbours' property three kilometres away. We stopped along the way, admiring the bluebells and pussy willows growing in the ditch. Our neighbours had a beautiful horse that waited for us at the edge of the fence. We never met those neighbours, but I saw the woman look out the window at us every time we visited.

I crawled through the barbed-wire fence and brushed the flies off the horse I named Sparklingeyes. She was gentle and beautiful, deep tan with black hair. We fed her our goodies out of the wagon and I vowed to her that, one day, I would take her away and she would be mine. My favourite book back then was *Black Beauty*, but to this day I have never ridden a horse.

These were the happiest days of my childhood. I spent every waking hour in the trees. I made mud pies with my mom's best pots, declared myself the leader of the yard with my sidekick sisters as we caught salamanders, saw a stick bug for the first time, ripped the legs off daddy-long-legs, got too close to wolf spiders, and watched a mischief of mice run through the tall grass when the combines came dozing down the fields. My fondest memories are from this home, even the memory of getting a strand of wheat lodged in my throat. I wanted to be like the men in movies who perched on wooden fences with wheat hanging from between their lips. My mother put peanut butter down my throat so the sharp edges wouldn't cut my insides as she pulled the strand out.

Talking with my mother later in life, I learned that her most unhappy memories are from this time. While I was writing songs about the trees and the sky, and the clouds drifting on by, my mother was inside, with our father.

YISKIPĀO is when the water rises, and I cannot help but wonder about the water that floats above us every day, powerful and invisible and on its way to form a cloud. How strange that something happens right in front of us, right on top of us, yet we cannot see it. At least not truly. There may be indicators, but even then, not everyone will see.

Next door to the acreage there lived a little girl named Anna. I was in the bedroom I shared with my sisters and we concocted a plan.

Orleane motioned to me. "You go."

"No, you go!" I retorted.

"I don't wanna ask him."

"I did it last time," Chayla chimed in.

"We know he's just gonna say no," I said.

"Just go and ask Mom. You're the better talker," Orleane told me.

"Fine, I'll go."

So I walked down the hallway and up the two steps that led into the living room. Mom was sitting in the armchair and Dad was on the couch. "Mom, can we go to Anna's to see if she can come play?" I asked.

Dad cocked his head. "No. You're not allowed."

I stared at him, black eyes on black eyes, locked. "Was I talking to you?"

His nostrils flared, but he was predictable in many ways. I knew he wouldn't let my mother decide, and I also knew that at the age of eight, I was tired of his tyranny. He clenched his fists, as he often did, and dragged me into the kitchen.

Sometimes it was a wooden spoon with the threat of the belt.

This time he opened the drawer and took out the belt.

After Dad was done with my punishment we were confined to the bedroom. I didn't understand why he was like that; I just knew it wasn't fair. My sisters and I sat in the room, angry that once again our lives were dictated by his moods.

I'll teach him he can't be our ruler.

It was a beautiful summer day outside. I stripped down, butt naked. I always hated the confines of fabric on my skin. We pushed a chair up to the window and I outlined our escape. My sisters looked at me like I was nuts and said they were staying inside. They encouraged my act of defiance, though. So I opened the window and popped out the screen. I looked down and saw a laundry vent coming off the side of the trailer. I hopped down onto it, and then felt the grass beneath my feet. I inhaled deeply—the scent of earth and laundry sheets filled my nostrils.

My body tingled and I began to run.

I ran up the yard in front of the big bay window.

I ran back down the side of the trailer, past the well, and into the birch trees.

Catch me, I dared him in my mind.

Eventually, my little legs found their way to our swing set and I hopped up, bare ass to the seat. I pushed forward, and backward, forward, backward, while my sisters watched from the window, waiting for the clenched fist to fall.

Wind is a sweet flavour. It is not bitter, and it is not cold. It flows across the land, glimpsing places we dream of, stealing their flavours as it grazes past. If you find a quiet place at the top of a hill and open your mouth, you can feel it lick you.

I swung

and swung

and swung

and each time gravity took me through its parabola, I opened my mouth wide. I let my tongue fall out and welcomed the wind. As the wind tickled me, laughter erupted from my belly in triumph. Dad could try to steal my light with his enveloping darkness, but the wind never allowed me to dull.

After I was finished with my swing of defiance, I hopped off, walked back to the window, placed my foot upon the vent, and hoisted myself up.

If Anna had been looking out her window, she would have seen my bare ass toppling inside.

WUSKOOWUN is when something lowers, when it is clouded, and my father tended to be just that—those darkened clouds that move quickly and hover low so that if you reach out your little fingers, you think you can touch them, but you can never really touch them, and don't you know that people are never as simple as the worst things they do?

My dad was a beautiful man with the most beautiful hair. His hair was long, cascading down his back, and he always wore it in a braid. My mom says I have his wavy chestnut curls. I also have his eyes, mouth, and woodpecker cheekbones. She also says I have his charisma and his power to make anyone believe anything.

He could have changed the world, but instead, he changed mine. He changed all of ours. He was a warrior to be feared, snaring rabbits and bringing moose home from the bush. I can picture the man he would've been in the old days, before the colonizers took over our land. He would've been the strongest warrior in our tribe, especially because his great-great-grandpa was Chief Peeaysis of the Peeaysis band. He would have led battles, the same way Chief Peeaysis led the men to fight in the North-West Rebellion, despite the government's threat to revoke their treaty status. My dad would have protected our people in the exact same way. He was a leader when he spoke, enchanting whoever was listening. A natural persuader. He would have made speeches that ended wars and brought courage when it was time to fight them. It was a gift he was born with and perhaps inherited from our ancestors, from Chief Peeaysis.

I like to believe that in one of his lifetimes, this was one of his truths.

In this lifetime, although he led a gang of drug dealers, he still embodied those traits. Earning respect, in his own dysfunctional way, in his own dysfunctional community.

In prison, he earned the nickname Killer because when he first went in, some guys came after him and he laid them all out, easy as breathing. His fury, his anger, when unleashed, silenced everything for miles.

All my fleeting memories of my father from the acreage are of his anger, or of me in his shadow. In one strong memory, my sisters and I were in the backseat of the car, my mom was in the front, and my dad was in the driver's seat. We were in some kind of work yard. This was years before my dad started selling drugs, or rather, this was one of the stints when he had a trades job. Our dog, Buddy, had just died after getting hit by a car in front of our property. My mother broke the news to my father and I watched a flood of sadness wash over his eyes, but only for a second, until he covered it with anger.

He punched the steering wheel over and over and over, and then hopped out of the car, slamming the door shut. He paced in front of our vehicle, kicking the gravel road, screaming, and punched some kind of shed. I couldn't understand why he was so angry at us about what happened to Buddy. We all loved him too. The silence in the car on the way home was palpable.

Today, a part of me wants to hug that man, the small kid inside him, whatever it was that told him anger was the only acceptable expression of sadness.

PAWOSIMEW means she scarcely sees him, as if through fog or thick bush, and isn't it so peculiar when something or someone is right in front of you, yet you cannot fully see them or hold them or grasp them, and who is the person who is veiled in the fog of a valley? Perhaps if we take a deep breath and blow as hard as we possibly can, like when we make a wish over our birthday cake, we will uncover the being behind the fog.

My dad's pinky finger was sawed in half and he always wore a gold ring on it. The finger beside it carried a bulky gold ring too, moulded into the shape of a bear's face. I thought his half a pinky finger was still stronger than the full one of other dads. He was the coolest person I knew, and his mangled pinky made him all the more significant, unique. All the more powerful, like a real bear in the wild carrying his wounds like a weapon.

When I was six years old I watched his hands press globs of colourful dough into moulds, showing me how to gently pull them out so the design remained pressed onto the dough.

"Dad, why is your pinky so small?" I held up mine to compare.

"Wah, this thing?" He wiggled it in the air. "Your daddy bear was workin' hard one day, and then the saw just cut it clean off."

"Ouch! Did it hurt?!"

"Pfft! Maybe for most dads, but I'm not like most, am I?" He gave me a wink.

I was wearing a Looney Tunes pyjama set, and he had

on a white Tasmanian Devil tank top. We matched as we worked side by side, tapping into our creative sides in tandem. I licked my finger before pressing it to my chin to admire my masterpiece, the salt from the dough lingering on my tongue. He looked over my work and admired its beauty, proud of the way my dough held the design intact, and the way I had learned so quickly. He and I would often do crafts together and I would watch his hands delicately stroke the pencil crayons back and forth within the lines of the colouring book or within the lines of his own drawings. I watched and copied, taking special care to never colour outside the lines, wanting my strokes to be as seamless as his.

He was a meticulous man in many ways, and this trait also came alive during the holidays.

Christmas was Dad's favourite holiday. I never saw him get angry during this season. Christmas morning was my favourite morning of all, but not because of any presents. I would wake up to our house filled with the smell of Dad's bannock. In Alberta, us Crees bake bannock in the oven; if we cook it in oil, then we call it fry bread. He made his bannock extra special by adding bacon and green onions to it, a tradition I practise to this day.

He loved this time of year more feverishly than I have ever seen him love anything. A month before, he would begin decorating the house with lights and trinkets. He was a perfectionist, and he always lit our tree with his careful hand, methodically taking his time as he wove the strings of coloured lights around each branch.

When Dad was gone, it was me who took on this responsibility.

When Dad was gone, it was me who baked the bannock.

When Dad was gone, it was me who mowed the lawn.

When Dad was gone, I shovelled the sidewalk.

When he was gone, I took out the trash.

When he was gone, I fixed what was broken.

My mom and my sisters and I laughed at how I had become the man of our household. Truthfully, I enjoyed the solitary act of these chores. I loved putting in the earbuds to my Discman or MP3 player and pushing the mower up and down the lawn in perfectly straight lines. The satisfaction that came along with the instant gratification—it was the same feeling as shovelling the snow. Sometimes, I think it made me feel closer to him, because even when he was still around, I loved to help him with these chores.

I just wanted to be near him.

After Dad was done with the lights, it would be time for us to hang the decorations. It was tradition for each of us girls to hang our special ornament. We each had one that we'd gotten on our first birthday, and once we were old enough, it was our duty to hang it on the tree. After the special ones were hung, we joined in to hang the rest. Dad always placed the star on the top.

Afterward, we sat in front of the tree as a family, basking in the ambiance of Christmas and drinking hot chocolate with tiny marshmallows floating on top.

In these moments, everything felt right. When I close my eyes and picture us as a family—the image of what a family is "supposed" to look like—these are the memories I conjure. These are the ones I let steep, but I can't steep them for too long, because after a moment, they turn bitter.

One Christmas morning, Chayla woke me and Orleane up at 5 a.m. Mom and Dad let us open our stockings before they woke up, but then we had to return to our beds until at least eight. We crept down the hall and began unearthing our goodies from our giant red socks that hung above the wood-burning fireplace. Inside, we always had a chocolate orange, a toothbrush, and a booklet of LifeSavers and Jolly Ranchers.

Dad hid a tiny present for each of us girls in the tree, usually a trinket or small piece of jewellery.

I regret selling all of them to buy drugs and alcohol when I was fourteen.

"Should we peek in the tree to see if we can spot what he got us?" Chayla asked.

"No way!" I said. "We have to leave it for a surprise!"

Orleane jokingly began to poke around at the tree.

"Stop!" I pushed her hands away. "We should get back to bed anyways." I laughed.

We marched back to our bedroom, carrying our little packets of candy.

A while later, I smelled cheddar baking in Dad's bannock, and when I bounded out of my room and into the kitchen, I saw venison from his hunt earlier in the winter thawing on the counter to be turned into stew. He was an exceptional cook, even though he didn't cook often, and I loved to watch him in the kitchen, jovial and serious and always with a bead of sweat on his forehead that he wiped periodically on his arm.

THEY SAY FAIRY TALES begin with once upon a time, but what I am about to tell you is not a fairy tale—what I am about to tell you happened under the sapphire chill of a blue moon.

Deep in the woods of the boreal forest, where the frost never leaves the forest floor, lived a young boy with the gift of the eyes. This young boy was only six years old, and he was known as Little Warrior. As the chief's son, he had great expectations placed upon him, and his shoulders were broad and large, even back then, to help him carry all his burdens. His gift, the one of sight, helped not just him but the whole tribe. When he closed his eyes each night, the Creator gifted him with visions of what was to come.

One night, amid the first great chill in the frosted forest, Little Warrior slept in his teepee all alone. His father had left to lead the Great Moose Hunt. One day, it would be up to Little Warrior to lead the Great Moose Hunt and protect the tribe from the Blackfoot over the mountains. The Blackfoot men were obsessed with Cree women and would sneak into their camps at night, stealing away the most beautiful Cree women from the tribe.

To this day, there are powerful Creefoot women, descendants of these raids, possessing the power of both Cree and Blackfoot lineages.

Little Warrior slept alone because his mother had to join his father on this particular hunt. Her name was Soapberry Paws because of the healing quality in her hands. She was the great medicine woman for the tribe and for all the neighbouring ones for miles.

Little Warrior had a vision that his mother would be needed on the Great Moose Hunt under the blue moon, and so she went—a testament to the trust placed in Little Warrior's visions.

So, under the forest chill on the night of the blue moon, Little Warrior slept, and he slept as deep as the mountains are high.

Beneath his soil-rich eyes, he saw himself as a grown man. He was crouched beside a lake with only the moon's glow illuminating his chestnut skin. His head rested in his palms as his fingers pulled at his hair so intensely he was almost ripping it from his scalp. The man was weeping. Little Warrior slowly approached his older self until he was standing just behind the man's shoulders. He reached out to touch him, and in that moment of connection, he stared at the man's reflection in the lake to realize it wasn't a man at all. Staring back at him from the water was the head of a man, no lips, with razor-sharp canines dripping blood, and from the top of his head grew antlers that reached wide and white for the moon. When Little Warrior touched the shoulders of his older self, crouched beside the lake, the creature laughed and laughed and laughed. Little Warrior shook violently until he awoke in the teepee, fire out, shivering underneath his hides.

His soul did not feel right. There was a chill inside him that had not been there before, something dark burning like an ember in the pitch black of a winter night. He stood up, noticed a tuft of animal hair near the fire, tossed it in the pit, and started the fire again. The hair burned up, a roaring azure. Then Little Warrior crawled back under the hides and into a dreamless sleep.

WUSKOWAGINUM is when he moves it, but it shouldn't be confused with wuskowagumipuyew, because that is a water that moves on its own, like when the particles dance high above and form amid the sky—my father was the one to redirect these bodies when we moved to the city when I was nine years old.

As we drove away from our home on the acreage, I looked back out the car window and said, "You can take the girl out of the country, but you can never take the country out of the girl."

We moved into a white barn-style home with three red stripes painted across its entirety on the north side of Edmonton, right off 118th Avenue in Westwood. The house was built in the early 1900s in an old wartime neighbourhood. My new elementary school was St. Patrick, and it was the first Catholic school I had ever attended; it eventually shut down because of severe underfunding. I stood each morning and recited "Hail Mary" and "Our Father."

One time a girl named Molly trapped me in the bathroom, barricading the door with her body and a ruler she was threatening to hit me with. She started pulling out her eyelashes, trying to coax me to join her. I feigned pulling out my eyelashes until I suddenly ripped the ruler out of her hand, shoved her to the floor, and ran full speed back to my classroom, where I told the teacher.

I often think of Molly and her twin brother, Matthew. They were very troubled young kids, and I can't help but wonder what must have been happening in their home to make them act out the way they did. I remember feeling as if they had some demonic quality to them, both pale like the Pakakos, black-haired, dark circles around their eyes, and mean. Really mean.

Molly used to ride the overhead glider on the playground to the other side, and then post up there, not allowing any of us other kids to have a turn. One time, I yelled at Molly from the other side, telling her she needed to send the glider back so the rest of us could play. She whipped the glider back as hard as she could, and it smacked me dead centre in the forehead. It knocked me out cold and I came to with a teacher and young kids all staring down at me.

In the white barn home I had a dream that my dad bought a new black SUV. When I woke up the next day, my dad came barrelling through the door, jingling keys in the air as we all watched.

"Look what I got today! Come outside!" Sitting in the driveway was a new black SUV.

"Dad! I dreamed about this last night! I knew this would happen."

He picked me up in his big brown arms. "A little dreamer we have here, don't we? This is a special power you have, my girl. Don't ever lose it. You always listen to the little voice inside that guides you. Okay?"

"Will do!"

He put me down. "How about we go for a ride?"

"Yes!"

OWIKAST'ĀTIN is when it is in the shade, it makes a shadow, or it is clouded, and it was at this home, during this era, that I recall the shadow building, like a cloud you don't realize is obstructing something beautiful from view. Something was shifting inside of me, inside all of us.

When I think of this home, I think of crying on the top bunk. One night, my mom was tucking me into bed and I started to cry.

"Mom, why does Dad love Orleane more than me?" I asked.

"Aw, my girl, he doesn't." She caressed my head. "He loves you all equally." She called my dad into the room and told him what I'd said.

He hugged me. "Wah, I love you so much, Chy-Chy. You're all my favourite."

But I didn't believe him.

After this, my dad started confiding in me.

He made me feel special and loved.

And when I think of this home, I think of ghosts. One time, my two cousins and their parents came to visit.

Orleane and I shared a room and it was in the basement. We had one of those bunk beds with a double on the bottom and a twin on the top. My uncle and aunt slept on the bottom bunk and I slept on the top with my cousin Jasmine. The basement was unfinished, which meant the floor was concrete.

I can still picture the morning light shining through the small barred window. An angled, striped shadow painted on the cold, grey concrete; dust particles floated in the air as if gravity didn't weigh them down, as if that basic law didn't apply to them.

The first night my relatives were sleeping on the bottom bunk, they woke me and my cousin by yelling at us. "What the hell are you girls doing?! Get to bed! You are not supposed to be out of the bed playing with your toys!"

"What are you talking about?" I asked groggily. "We were sleeping." As we lazily rubbed our eyes, I saw that my toys were now out of the closet and strewn all over the floor.

My uncle and aunt were stunned. "Oh ... we heard voices ... Well, just go back to sleep." My aunt got up and put all the toys back in the closet.

Then there was the time Orleane woke up in the middle of the night and saw a family standing at the foot of our bed. Before I moved into the basement, my sisters and I shared the bedroom upstairs across the hall from my parents. Orleane described the man as looking like Abraham Lincoln, and there was a mother holding a baby, a little boy, and a little girl who ran out of the room. Orleane shook me, but by the time I woke up, they were gone.

Another time when we were sleeping in that room, Dad got up in the middle of the night to yell at us. He said he had woken up to the TV being turned on and off and heard little kids playing Ring Around the Rosie in the living room. We woke up to my father yelling angrily and stomping around naked, only for him to stop abruptly once he saw that we were all tucked into bed. That was the first time I remember seeing a man's naked body. The first time I was aware that a man's naked body was not for my child eyes to see.

One of these memories stands out the most, perhaps because we were all together. We were all on the couch in the living room having a family movie night. We had gone to Blockbuster and picked out a movie and all our favourite snacks. Mine and my father's was Clodhoppers. Before we all snuggled up together, we cleaned the whole house. My mom washed the dishes, and she had these massive A&W mugs drying on the innermost part of the counter. They were classic, thick mugs that we would make root beer floats in. As we were watching the film, we heard a loud smash in the kitchen. My dad got up to have a look, and sure enough, one of the mugs had flown off the counter and smashed into thousands of pieces all over the floor. The strangest part was that even if you dropped one of those mugs, it wouldn't break because of how thick it was.

As we grew older, we uncovered more of these stories. My mom told me of the time she was napping on the couch when she heard the back door unlock and someone come inside and go down the stairs. She assumed we must have gotten home early from school and called to us but was met with silence. She went to the back door and saw that it was still locked, and no one else was home.

Perhaps the scariest memory in that house was from my ninth birthday. I had about seven girls over from school and my dad was in the backyard grilling. We were all downstairs in my bedroom playing ghost tag, where the person who's "it" wears a blindfold. My friend Nicole was "it" and we all got a sneaky idea to hide on the top bunk. As we were quietly giggling, watching her wander around slowly with her arms outstretched, she suddenly grabbed on to thin air as if she'd captured one of us.

"I got you!" she yelled excitedly, but when she was about to take off her blindfold, it looked like she got pushed over onto the ground. We all started yelling and quickly climbed down from the bunk bed. We grabbed Nicole and ran outside. We told my parents what had happened and Nicole said, "It felt like someone pushed me over and then stepped on my arm." We all could see that her arm was red, a bruise forming.

All my dad said was, "Well, maybe you girls should just play outside for a bit. Hot dogs will be ready soon anyways."

US CREES, we have two important ceremonies when someone dies: the wake and the round dance. These ceremonies deliver the body back to the Earth Mother and allow the spirit to pass on, ascending into the spirit realm. They are an essential part of the bereavement and healing processes.

The wake can last up to four days and three nights. All the friends, family, and relatives of the deceased take turns staying with the body. We share stories and memories from the person's life. We cry, but we also laugh, as both are medicines that help our souls through our grief. We sing and offer prayers. The women prepare the food throughout the wake, and the intention of the feast is to eat with the spirits, as we believe all the ancestors and spirits gather around, ready to hold the hand of the newly deceased as they move into the spirit realm.

To help the spirit undo their ties to the physical world and all they held on to within it, we are not to cry during the fourth night. After a year has passed, we hold a feast—the potlatch, honouring the passage of the spirit from the body.

Neither the spirit nor their people ever truly part from one another.

But there has always been a distinction between a ghost and a spirit.

A spirit is a soul that has passed on to the other side, having released its ties to the physical body and the physical realm.

A ghost is a soul who holds on.

A ghost is a soul who may have died suddenly, tragically, or without proper burial.

When I think of the white barn home, or the other places where I have felt a ghost, I think of what those ghosts might still be holding on to. Or who has buried them anonymously, without ceremony, without ritual, left them there without a hope of ever being found.

If we find them—can we send them home?

WHEN LITTLE WARRIOR awoke, he did not tell anyone of his dream, not this one. There was something private about it, something sinister—something that scared him to his bones. What Little Warrior did not know was that fear was the gasoline that fuelled the dark little ember burning inside of him, and his silence made it grow and grow until it absorbed him, pulsing beneath his flesh.

When his parents returned from the Great Moose Hunt, the bounty was abundant. They had secured enough meat to last through the winter, and even extra to trade with neighbouring tribes.

When Soapberry Paws asked Little Warrior what he had dreamed while they were away, all he told her was that he had dreamed of a great bounty for the winter. Soapberry Paws ruffled his hair, acknowledging the power and truth of his visions.

As Little Warrior grew older, he learned to hunt just like his father and absorbed the lessons of ancient plant medicine from his mother, but his dreams had taken on a life of their own. His dreams had become a breeding ground for darker spirits. He often saw the ghost-like spectre of the Pakakos, flying above the forest, seeking its victims. He often saw himself by the dark lake. That dream was always the same, and as time went on, the goodness in Little Warrior seeped out of his blood, one small act of violence at a time.

But he kept his violences out of sight.

One night, in the teepee with his mother and father, he came to find himself awake, standing over his father, hands hovering above his scalp. He did not remember waking, but here he was. He saw the visions beneath his father's eyes: His mother squirmed underneath his father, whose hands were wrapped around her neck.

Little Warrior was not so little anymore, and above anyone else, he loved his mother.

One night, Little Warrior and his father set out on a hunt. They were deep in the thick brush when they spotted a moose up ahead. Both of them moved silently, bows arched and ready. The moment his father released his arrow into the moose, Little Warrior also released his—straight into his father's heart. His father looked back at him; confusion and betrayal poured from his eyes. Little Warrior walked toward him and dug the arrow in deeper, until his father's heart took its last beat. After, Little Warrior tended to the moose, removed the antlers, and dug them deep into the wound from the arrow.

It was time to go back to the tribe.

TAHKIPESTAW is when cold rain falls, and the next home was the place where the rain hung in the air at the edge of the clouds, waiting for release.

This was the home where I learned the secret of an adult.

The unravelling was beginning, slow at first, before it quickened to the pace of no return. It wasn't a shift like the white barn home; it was more like an extraction. An extraction of what once was and a replacement with what my father created. His woven world of manipulations.

The white duplex in Rosslyn on the north side of Edmonton. My parents waited for more than a year to get us into the Métis Capital Housing Corporation, a low-income housing development for Indigenous people. It was small but the biggest place we had ever lived: a three-bedroom with a semi-finished basement. The first place where we each had our own bedroom.

Chayla was in grade one, I was in grade five, and Orleane was in grade eight. I went to St. Matthews and it was the fourth school I had attended, stuck in the cycle of being the new kid, making and letting go of friends.

We celebrated our last Christmas together as a family there. Perhaps on some level we were preparing for a new era, a new chapter in our lives.

That Christmas Eve, we ordered Chinese food, and while we were waiting for it to arrive, it was time to open one gift. Every year, my mom handed each of us girls our presents and we opened them at the same time.

I got a pink pyjama set and Shel Silverstein's *Where the Sidewalk Ends.* My sisters each got their own pyjamas and books. We watched *Olive, the Other Reindeer,* which was one of our favourites.

It was getting late, so we finished our spring rolls and chow mein and went to bed. This time, we could hear our parents wrapping presents and we knew Santa Claus wasn't real. We slowly crept out of our bedroom, taunting our parents, trying to catch them in the act. Soon enough, they said, "Fine! You caught us. Get out here!"

"Can we open the rest of our presents now?" The three of us girls pleaded in unison. "Please, please, please!"

They caved and we opened all our presents at midnight.

There's a photo of me in my pink pyjamas and a thick black punk-rock choker, listening to the new Sum 41 album on a Discman. Even though this was the last time we all celebrated Christmas together, my mother, my sisters, and I carried on this new tradition of opening all our presents at midnight on Christmas Eve, without my dad.

It seemed like a miracle for all of us to be together for Christmas, because a year prior, shortly after we had moved into the duplex, my parents had separated.

Years later, my mother told me the story. That day, Chayla stayed home sick from school. When my mom got home from her shift at Financial Stop there was Dad, sitting on the living room floor, playing Xbox. She told me it was as though thirteen years of pent-up rage at the abuse that happened behind closed doors and out of sight bubbled over. She ripped the console from the wall and threw it right at his head.

She saw his eyes flicker and his black pupils take over. He leaped up and punched her in the head, and she punched him right back. He grabbed her by the collar and wrestled her to the ground. He slammed her on the carpet a few times as she fought back. With the last blow he gave her, she felt her consciousness waver, and she gave up. She stopped fighting because she knew if she didn't, she might end up dead. They looked at each other—neither was moving. She got up, went to the bathroom, and saw blood on her head. She went into the bedroom and found Chayla hiding. She took her to get ice cream, and then to the park.

Chayla looked up at her and said, "I heard one loud bang, and then it was quiet. I thought you died."

In that moment, my mom knew it was over. She was leaving him.

At that time I didn't know my dad was dealing drugs, but after my mom left him, he ventured deeper into the drug world, immersed further in the land of lost souls.

For months, my dad tormented her.

She woke up one morning and her tires were slashed. One night she and her best friend, Charm, who is also my dad's cousin, were out drinking at the bar. My dad and his friend showed up and said they would take them to a bush party. She and Charm left with them, and my dad drove farther and farther out of the city.

Out of the blue, he slammed on the brakes, turned around, and drove back into the city.

"Where are we going?" my mom asked.

"I'm taking you girls home."

His friend dated Charm and later told her that my dad was driving them out there to kill them. He was going to shoot them and leave their corpses in the country.

For some reason, he changed his mind.

MESCIPICIKEWIN is when something fully absorbs the water, and it also means picking all the berries, and these two things seem so disjointed that they couldn't possibly share the same word, but they do and it's because they both embody the idea of leaving nothing behind. All the liquid is absorbed and all the berries have been picked; there is now a deficiency of nutrients—a leaching has occurred.

After my parents separated, my sisters and I split our time between them, one week with each parent, and my dad used his time strategically.

Our whole lives we'd never had more than we needed. We'd always shopped for clothing at Walmart or the Salvation Army. When we lived on the acreage, I didn't think much about what I was wearing because I mostly destroyed all my clothes, and chances were I was going to whip them off at some point anyway.

But when we moved into the city, this changed. In grade five I started noticing a difference in the way other kids dressed compared to the way I dressed. I suddenly wanted cooler jeans, purses, makeup, trendy designer shirts. There were these jeans that all the other girls had. I remember going back-to-school shopping with my mom—the first time we went shopping in a mall instead of at Walmart or Zellers. We went to Garage and I begged her to buy them. My mom saw the price tag and said, "Forty dollars?! I'm sorry, my girl, but we just can't afford that."

"But please, Mom?! All the other kids have nicer clothes than I do. I'll take good care of them," I promised.

I could see her contemplating, holding the jeans and calculating inside her head. "Okay ... well ... if you get these jeans, then you won't have that much to spend on shirts and things."

I knew she was changing her mind. "Thank you! That's okay!"

"You need to know, now that you're getting older, I can't afford to buy all the expensive clothes. Once you're old enough, you're going to have to get a job so you can pay for your own clothes if you want the expensive ones."

I took in what she said as we walked to the cashier. I longed for the day I would turn thirteen and could get a job to start buying all the things I wanted.

But when we went to stay with my dad, things were different from how I had ever known them to be. We would drive around in nicer cars, and every time he opened his wallet there would be stacks of cash. When we went to school, he would give us forty dollars each to pay for breakfast and lunch. We always got food delivery or went out to eat at Chili's or occasionally the Keg steakhouse. He took us shopping at the mall and bought us brand-name shoes, clothes, purses, everything.

He provided us with everything we longed for materialistically during a time in our lives when we naturally cared so much about fitting in, about what our peers thought of us. My dad's houses and possessions slowly became nicer and nicer, even though we never stayed in any one place for long, constantly moving, so much so that in the span of two years with our father after the separation, we lived in at least seven different places. Still, there is an allure to that consumerism when you've been accustomed to poverty.

My mother couldn't compete. She couldn't provide the same nice things that my dad could.

One day I was in his car with him and I asked, "Dad, how do you make money? All I see is you driving around all the time."

"I'll tell you something, but you gotta keep it to yourself."

"Okay, promise."

"Your dad is gonna be an undercover cop soon."

I felt important because he let me in on his secret. I was special. Each time I saw him, he would whisper little "facts" in my ear, and I believed him. I never suspected that my own father would lie to me. I worshipped him, and I felt special because he spoke to me like I was an adult.

Once he told me, "Your mom cheated on me with many guys. That's why we're not together anymore." I believed that during the week we were away from her my mom was using drugs, partying every night, and hooking up with random guys from the bar. I once saw a straw in her car and took that as evidence of something she would use to snort cocaine.

He fed me lies about her, and I ate them up.

I started to resent her.

Amid that resentment, I grew closer and closer to my father.

PIKIHTEWATÂMIW is when his breath is visible, like a vapour in the cold air, and what I love the most about this word is that a presence cannot be hidden; it conjures stories of ghosts in the forest and the idea of being haunted, and even then, even there, the breath like vapour in the cold air is always there for you to see—the opposite of an unveiling, but a reveal nonetheless.

I don't think my dad ever sat me down and told me that he was a drug dealer, but there were clues that something different was happening with him. It was a slow normalization. When you're inside of something, when it's all you've ever known, it's hard to see it clearly for what it is.

The first time I ever saw crack cocaine it was sitting in mounds on my kitchen table. I was ten years old and my dad showed Orleane and her friend and me how to weigh and bag it. He left to sell drugs, and we sat there, weighing and bagging.

I knew how to turn cocaine into crack when I was in grade seven. I used to wonder what my dad was doing in the kitchen with a tin cup inside a metal pot. I remember the bead of sweat above his eyebrow and him yelling at me to get back into my room. It was like a game to see how much I could learn, how much I could take in, before being banished to my bedroom once again. Kids take in their surroundings in only a few seconds.

When he picked us up from school, it would take hours to get home. He would grab McDonald's for us, and then we would drive by people; sometimes he would chuck something out the window at them, and I cannot count on both hands how many times crackheads said, "Wow, your daughters are so beautiful." I have a memory of being with him and his friend in the front seat as we drove down

118th Avenue and yelled profanities at the drug addicts and prostitutes.

Dad was a big and powerful drug dealer and I inherited that false sense of power. In grade seven, I ran my mouth, because who was going to fuck with me? No one. I was becoming more and more like my father. I started getting into fights, saving my lunch money to buy weed and, eventually, cigarettes and alcohol. I inherited the way he talked down to people, and I knew how to fight because he taught me. One look from my dad was all it took to make someone step down, and I knew that well.

I admire my mother for never stepping down from him.

I used to memorize every place that I drove to with my dad out of a fear that if I needed to escape, I would know how to get back home on foot. Even though I wasn't fully aware of what I was fearing, I could feel that something was unsafe. At some point my dad told us that we couldn't tell anyone what he did or the police would take him away and we wouldn't be able to see him again. All I knew was that I loved my father, and I wanted to stay with him. Better the devil you know.

When I was in grade six, my dad got caught selling crack outside our apartment building. He had gotten up early that morning and told me he had errands to run.

"But you promised today would be a family day," I said. We were supposed to go to the West Edmonton Mall water park.

"It will. I'll be home around noon, and then we'll go."

"Fine. I'll be waiting. I'll let the girls know."

He looked at me as he was heading out the door.

"Dad?"

"Yes, my girl?"

"If you fuck this up, I'll never forgive you."

"Wah, you think you're the dad now or what?" He ruffled my hair.

The day was overcast and I sat on the spiral staircase that led to the lower floor where our bedrooms were. I held my flip phone as I waited for my dad to call. It was 11:30 a.m. and I hadn't heard from him. My stomach was in knots. My heart was quickening and my stomach was curdling. I flipped open my cell and called him.

"Dad, you need to come home."

"It's not even noon yet. I still have some things to do."

"Dad, listen to me. Something bad is going to happen to you."

"Nothing bad is going to happen. I promise, okay? But I'll be a little late. I'll be there for two o'clock. Make sure your sisters are ready."

I started to cry. "Dad, listen! Just come home!"

"Don't cry. It's gonna be fine. I'll be home as soon as I can, okay?"

I sat on the spiral staircase and didn't move. I couldn't shake the feeling. I sat in my bathing suit and shorts and waited, but I knew, one way or another, we wouldn't be making it to the water park that day. At half past one I called my dad over and over again, but he didn't answer.

I went into the room I shared with Orleane. "I think something bad happened to Dad. He's not answering the phone. Can you try to call him from your phone?"

"I'm sure he's fine. Who cares?" She sat in front of the mirror, applying lip gloss.

"Orleane, please just try to call him!"

"Fine, don't be such a freak."

He didn't pick up. I paced up and down the staircase, unable to think about anything else.

Why didn't he listen to me?

When the cops booted down our apartment door, a stroke of luck saved my sisters and me from being sent to child protective services (CPS).

Many children are not so lucky, especially Indigenous children.

Indigenous children make up about 7 percent of the Canadian population, yet they account for 52 percent of children in the foster care system. It is rare for CPS to give Indigenous children back to their parents.

A childhood friend of my mom's happened to drive by as my dad was being handcuffed outside the building. She phoned my mom, who pulled up within minutes.

She called me and said, "Your dad is getting arrested. You have two minutes to pack as much as you can and get out back—NOW!"

My sisters and I threw our clothes into duffle bags. As soon as we got out the door, down the back stairs, and into my mom's car, our apartment was raided by the police and social services.

Dad served six months for drug trafficking, and we miraculously escaped joining our fellow Indigenous children in the system.

Daddy loves you Chyana
Chyana Marie Sage I love you plus miss you to
Happy days will be ours again
You are the life of my love
Always and forever
Never ever will this happen again
Always together until the end

Missing you forever
Always
Remember Chyana
I love you
Empty without you Chyana I love you

Supper I will cook for you um it is so good
Always tasty my food so good I will bake for us to.
Giggling and laughing catching up with time
Empty i feel without you I love and miss you to

Logan is your name forever it will be
On my word my little bumble bee
Going on forever
Always my love to be
Never ever to hurt you Chyana Marie I miss you

I Logan love you, your daddy every day

Loving you forever
Opening our hearts forever and ever
Violets are blue and sweet as you
Everyday daddy will be thinking of you

U R FOREVER Chyana Marie Sage Logan I love you, daddy

PÚKOOPÃO is when he goes into the water, but it was more than that; he was fully submerged in the way that a human would float within a cloud, drowning in the very air around him.

I went to visit my father in prison and the perimeter of my hand started to fog, creating an outline like when chalk lines at a crime scene embody ghosts on pavement. He was serving time in the Edmonton Remand Centre for dealing crack outside our apartment building. I sat on a metal seat in a cold booth facing a pane of Plexiglas. My father entered the cubicle on the other side of the barrier. He placed his veiny brown hand on the glass and I brought mine up to mirror his. We waited for the red light to go on, signalling that we would now be able to hear each other. He picked up his phone and I picked up mine.

I was ten years old. I don't remember what we said, but I remember how small our phone booth was. I remember the way my small child's body was the perfect size for the tiny metal seat, and I wondered how my father, massive and brown and muscled, could possibly fit on his identical seat on the other side of the glass. I remember there were rows of identical cubicles on either side of us flowing down the wall—the demarcation between captivity and freedom.

Barriers between loved ones.

I remember he had tears in his eyes that he never let fall.

And I remember mine, puddling in my collarbone.

I remember feeling them drip slowly down my cheek,
my chin,
my neck,
losing themselves underneath my shirt.
I remember we had fifteen minutes.

When the buzzer rang I watched my dad's lips move, unable to hear what he was saying anymore.

Hand to glass.

While my dad sat in a cell, I sat in the basement of my mom's home and held a butter knife in one hand. My cheeks were swollen from my tears, and my eyes matched. I brought my fingers to my eyelids and pressed down gently. Press and release. I liked the way it felt when my fingertips touched my eye pillows.

Why didn't he listen to me? I'd told him I knew something bad was going to happen. I could feel it. I can always feel it.

I grabbed the sharpener from my pencil case. With the butter knife I carefully took out the screw that held the blade in place in the plastic. Dropping the screw on the floor, I held the blade in my hand. I went to the bathroom and filled a small cup with hydrogen peroxide. I went back to the basement and sat on the green carpet. I watched the dirty blade send bubbles to the surface in the cup.

After the bubbles dissipated, I reached in and took out the blade. I rolled up my sleeves and looked at my soft brown skin. My eye pillows throbbed. Whoever said that sticks and stones may break your bones but words will never hurt you lied to you.

I think my father told me that.

Words smoke you behind the neck before diving period-first into your solar plexus.

Words wiggle their way inside your core and jump around, molesting your organs and wiping your memories clean.

Words keel you over and make you vomit.

Those words my mother spoke: "Your dad is getting arrested."

No, no, no! They can't take him away from me. He is MINE! My daddy bear. Fucking pigs. They ruin everything.

Emotional trauma gets stuck inside us and it needs to be released.

When I was in grade six, I did not know this—not in those terms.

Everything was rattling, my fingers trembled, and my eyes blurred because the salt spirits were with me. My tears wouldn't leave me alone for a fucking second! *Leave me ALONE!* I gripped the blade harder and focused on the way it felt. It was wet and cold and hard. Very hard. But delicate. I pressed its point into my child-soft flesh and slowly applied more pressure until red oozed around it. I dragged it hard along the skin, and slowly the rattling in my head began to lessen.

My skin somehow held me together, and as I released the blade I watched the blood drip down the sides of my forearm. The sight of my blood calmed my nervous system. The blood was a reminder that I was there and I was real and what I felt on the inside was okay because it was still connected to the outside of my body.

The dancing of my organs ceased with the pull of the blade.

I was calm. The salt spirits left me alone, for a time.

SPIRALLED STAIRCASE

Small body
A glimpse into a bedroom

Pink precious bedsheets
Lacking innocence
Poignant sins

A large hand
Shutting the door
Only a glimpse

Of her pink stained eyes
While I spiralled
With the staircase

AFTER LITTLE WARRIOR killed his father, the whole tribe mourned the loss of their chief, but no one cried harder than Little Warrior, wailing each time someone's eyes glanced his way. The very next day, Little Warrior took on his new role as chief of the tribe. Everyone cheered for him, knowing he would try to be the best leader for them. And soon, the memory of his father faded further and further into the past.

Before long, it was time for Little Warrior to take a wife and have children.

There was a powerful Cree woman in their tribe. Her name was Pebble Dancer because she would often be found hopping and skipping along the pebbles by the river. Her wind-tousled hair cascaded behind her with each step she took, moving like the currents in the water. She was jovial but respected because she was the greatest hunter in the tribe—trained as a young girl by Little Warrior's own father. She was always destined for Little Warrior.

It did not take long for them to fall in love, and soon Pebble Dancer gave Little Warrior three children, all girls.

Little Warrior prayed each night for a son, but the Creator never gifted him with one. At night, his father would visit him, and Little Warrior's soul was tormented, never escaping the horrible thing he had done. This haunting turned Little Warrior harder and harder, until all his soft edges were gone. Not having a son felt like a punishment, and Little Warrior filled up with rage. Pebble Dancer did not know where the man she married had gone. Who was this dark man?

One night, while Little Warrior slept, Pebble Dancer lay beside him, unable to quiet her mind. The moonlight was strong and she heard a low grumble. Soft and quiet at first, until it grew louder, more powerful, into a full cry. It came from Little Warrior. She watched his chest heave, higher and higher, until his whole torso was levitating above their furs. Tears streamed down her face as she felt the air in the room grow cold and full, as if there was no more air left to breathe—as if the moon had died and the pitch black had swallowed them both whole.

Suddenly, Little Warrior fell back to the earth, but he did not wake; in fact, he did not seem to notice that anything had happened to him at all.

ISKUKOOTITOW is when he covers something with water, and in this moment he holds me under and never lets go.

Before my dad served time for drug dealing, he told me his secret. The biggest one of all. He and I went to the grocery store together. It was a warm day where the sun shone through a thin layer of grey clouds. We parked in the Safeway lot. The sepia-toned sunlight pierced the window, illuminating the dust particles floating in the car.

"Dad, wait."

His hand stopped reaching for the handle and he turned to look at me. "What is it? Wah, Wîsahkêcâhk got your tongue?"

"You treat Orleane differently from the way you treat me and Chayla. I see things, sometimes. Something is different."

He was quiet, staring at me. "Well, I have to tell you something, my girl," he began. "You can't tell your mother, because she won't understand. You'll understand, my little Chy-Chy. You know you have an old soul, right? Can I trust you to keep my secret?"

"Yes, you can. Just don't hide things from me."

"Well, you know that Orleane is not my biological child, right?"

"I know." I learned this when we lived on the acreage, when Orleane's biological father was dying in the hospital.

"Well, me and her are in love. Because I am not her real dad, this is why it's okay. When she turns eighteen, we're gonna get married. I'm gonna take you and Chayla and Orleane, and we're all gonna move to Ontario. I'll change my name. We're gonna start a new life, away from your mom. You know what a selfish bitch she is. She doesn't want your dad to be happy, and that's why you can't tell her. I'm telling you because I know how smart you are, and I know you'll understand. I can trust you. You want your dad to be happy."

I was nine years old. I was a daddy's girl, and he had been treating me as his confidant for years. I believed every word he told me.

Children are not born doubting their parents.

We learn every truth of this world through them.

PATOTECIWAN is when the river flows outside the riverbed; perhaps there is no avoiding that, in the way there never is, yet we humans still decide that next to the river is where we want to live.

Before I had to bury my father, when I was seven years old, we lived on an acreage with the evergreens surrounding it. We sat in a circle with the flames at our centre. Looking up at the sky, I saw the tips of the trees sway inward and outward, a little darker than the starlit sky. My two sisters sat on either side of me, my mother was across the fire to my right, and my father to the left. Looking up from my bare, scarred legs swinging back and forth below the wicker chair, I met his eyes. He looked back at me and the ember glow illuminated his high cheekbones, casting a shadow under his buffalo eyes.

My buffalo eyes.

The flames spat and crackled at my feet. He opened his mouth and his grave voice told stories of the Witigo.

I stood up to wander into the forest to pee. With a smile on his firelit lips, my dad called after me: "Make sure Witigo doesn't come get 'chu."

No, Dad, make sure he doesn't get you.

AFTER THAT NIGHT in the teepee, it seemed that darkness had taken full control of Little Warrior, except for small moments of love that would escape every now and again.

The children of Little Warrior and Pebble Dancer were growing, strong and fierce, each with her own gifts. The eldest daughter, a true empath who communicated mostly without having to speak. The youngest daughter, an avid plant medicine woman in the making. And the middle daughter, a warrior like both her mother and her father. No one knew that the middle daughter was also a dreamer, like her father. When she was a child, her grandfather visited her one night and told her to keep her gift to herself, so no one would try to take advantage of her.

When the middle daughter was young, she worshiped her father. She wanted to be just like him and demanded to learn everything he knew. She was the closest thing to a son for him—she had the strength of all the little boys in the village combined.

The whole tribe worshiped Little Warrior. He was a strong hunter, provider for the clan, and he always led them to victory in battle. But he was a different being when no one was watching. There were moments when the middle daughter thought she saw blood leaking from her father's eyes, but she would blink a few times and it was gone. As she grew, though, she began to resent him. She noticed the bruises on Pebble Dancer, and her dreams at night told her the reasons why.

She once had a dream of a little boy standing behind her father, or what appeared to be her father—a being with antlers reaching tall toward the moon. A glowing yellow aura surrounded the little boy. She watched him touch the antlered being's shoulders, and in that moment, the being's black aura took every ounce of light away from the little boy. This dream followed the middle daughter all her life.

Once, under the sapphire chill of a blue moon, the clan was slumbering blissfully in their lodgings. The middle daughter shared a teepee with her two sisters, and this night she was awakened by a voice calling her name within her dream: *Wanderer... Wanderer... WANDERER!* She woke to the icy air of the crisp forest floor and knew she had to leave her teepee. She was unaware of where she was heading, an invisible cord drawing her forward. As she slipped through her doorway and out into the frosted air, she grabbed her arrows.

One foot moved in front of the other, as if it wasn't her guiding them, and soon she saw a set of footprints. They were big and hoofed. Bigger than a moose—bigger than anything she had ever seen. She followed and, before long, she realized the footprints were headed toward her parents' teepee. She ran through the thin layer of snow. When she opened the flap, she saw a giant being taking a bite out of her mother's chest. Without missing a beat, the middle daughter drove her strongest arrow through the antlered beast's heart.

At the moment of connection, the antlers melted away, the fur disappeared, and lying beneath her was her father, Little Warrior, and in his eyes she saw the eyes of the little boy in her dream.

The room swelled as if darkness had taken form and suffocated all the air before bursting into a thousand fragments and out through the teepee opening toward the blue moon.

OHCHIKAWAPOWIN is the shedding of teardrops, and I can't help but wonder if the act of a tear falling is more like the formation of dew—the exact moment that the vapour transforms into liquid and emerges from the corner of an eye—or if it is more like the act of precipitation, falling immediately from the corner of the eye upon its emergence. Perhaps it is the precise moment when each process meets the other—the moment of intersection.

After Dad was released from prison, Orleane and I went to live with him. Because I was now twelve years old, I could choose which parent to live with, and I chose him. One day, my dad brought me into his bedroom. He said he had something important to tell me. First, he grabbed me by the breast and said, "Oh, look, you're developing."

I brushed him away. "Dad, stop."

That's when he told me. "You're going to be an aunt. Orleane is pregnant."

"So does that mean I will be an aunt or a sister?" I asked him.

He stared at me. "Whatever you prefer."

The rest of this memory is blank, empty, void.

Orleane was fifteen years old. She at first said it was some boy she went to school with, but our mother knew. When my dad was serving time for drug dealing, he wrote us girls letters and my mother opened them and read them first. Inside those letters to Orleane, my father professed his love for my older sister.

"What the fuck do you do when the man who raised your daughter, the man who changed her diapers, the man you loved for thirteen years, has abused his power and been molesting her?" my mother choked out to me over a decade later.

Back then, my mom sat at our kitchen table with my uncle Jason and her best friend, Charm. "What the fuck. Is this actually happening? Am I insane?"

My uncle Jason was silent, grave, his eyes almost black. "I don't know, Les. They're in the bedroom a lot and I don't know what's happening, but something doesn't seem right." He seemed tortured by the thought, haunted. He idolized his brother and didn't want to believe that he was capable of hurting his children, the way their own father had sometimes harmed them.

My mom confronted Frank. After we discovered what he had done, he was no longer my father in my eyes.

"You're fucking sick, Les," he accused her. "What the fuck had to happen to you to make you think this kind of fucked-up shit?"

Was he right? Was she so fucked up from her childhood that she was imagining it? Was the relationship really innocent? A voice inside her head screamed, *No. No. No.* She had heard that voice before, when Orleane was a baby, and that voice had told her, *Leave Frank, now!*

She didn't listen then. She loved him; in a way, it was that simple.

But now she took the letters to a couple of psychologists and one of them confirmed her worst nightmare. His name was Doctor Jim and he said, "These are not the letters of a father to a daughter. These are the letters of a sick man who is taking advantage of a little girl."

She took the letters to the police and they said there was nothing they could do.

"What the fuck do you mean you can't do anything?" She was outraged. "A full-grown man is raping a child, and there's nothing you can do?"

Frank always had this grandiose plan to change his name to Jordan Lee Stone, take me and my sisters, and move us all to Ontario. Because he signed the letters *Jordan Lee Stone,* the police told her that there was no incriminating proof.

She needed proof. For months my mother built a case against him.

A week or two before Orleane told my mom about the pregnancy, my mom got a sick feeling in her stomach. Chayla's school had called to say they were concerned for Chayla's well-being, because every time she stayed with her dad, she would show up to school without lunch, looking like she had barely slept. That day, my mom went to work, and then almost immediately told her boss she needed to leave. Fuck this, her kids were in trouble. She could feel it in every cell of her body.

She got in her car and started driving to the house where we were living with Frank. At the same time, Orleane called her and said, "Mom, come get us."

"I'm already on my way," she replied.

Orleane turned to look at me. "Mom is coming to get

us, pack your things. I don't think we'll be coming back here for a while."

"What do you mean we aren't coming back?"

"Chyana, just listen to me and pack your shit. Quickly."

I didn't understand what was happening, but I heard the desperation in my sister's voice. I didn't ask any more questions and did as she told me. I felt her urgency, the fear that Frank would arrive before our mom did.

Before long, our mother was outside and we were throwing our duffle bags, once again, into the back of her car. We stayed with her and weren't allowed to see him.

She called child protective services. "We will send someone over to your place tomorrow to interview your kids," they said. "Keep them home from school."

Tomorrow came and no one arrived. She called them. "No one showed up yet? They should be there," was the reply. "If not today, then tomorrow."

She kept us home another day.

They didn't show up for a second time, and my mother called again.

They told her no one would be coming.

My mother can't remember the excuse they gave her.

Mom called Grandma Thelma and they hired a private investigator. They went to meet this man at a restaurant on the north side of Edmonton.

He listened to my mother and shook his head slowly. "You'd be surprised at how often people call me for this exact reason. I've hid nanny cams in many houses for stories just like this one. We'll get what we need."

She got a device from him to record phone conversations.

Orleane was lying in bed.

She was always lying in bed.

Mom crawled in with her and said, "You know you can tell me anything."

Orleane just looked at her, silent.

"If it's too hard to say it out loud, you can write it down on this piece of paper." She took a notebook and placed it inside a basket with a pen.

Every day she checked that basket.

One time it looked like a couple pages had been ripped out.

She'd check the basket, and then lock herself in the bathroom and listen to the phone conversations she'd recorded.

She listened to Frank and me talk about how much we hated her for keeping him away from us. At the time, I still wasn't aware that Orleane did not want to be with him. I wasn't aware that everything I had been witnessing between them for the last four years was abnormal. It had been normalized to me for years. I was still just a little girl, who was a daughter, who saw the world through her father's cunning eyes.

Frank asked to speak with Orleane, so I went and got her.

She heard Orleane say, "No, no, please. Tell him I'm not home."

When she did talk to him, she made up excuses to get off the phone quickly. "Mom's home, I gotta go." Even though she wasn't.

One day, my mom heard it.

They were talking about the due date of the baby, and she heard it.

It was the proof she needed for the police.

She breathed silently as she listened to the recorded phone call. Some people make up rationalizations, explanations for the abysmal atrocities that find them. They want to believe that the people they know are not capable of being monsters.

I believe in monsters.

These are my ears, she told herself. *I am listening.*

It was all ringing, ringing, ringing. But she was hearing, make no mistake. She chose to be wide-eyed.

She did not choose the darkness.

She breathed quietly.

Undetectable.

Each noise a slice to the throat, tears streaming down her pinkened cheeks.

Silent.

But the voices droned on, horrific and true.

All too true.

The tears kept streaming.

She vibrated.

She sat on the front step and called her friend Ken. That's when she saw Frank parked on the corner. She got up and started chasing his car. He drove past, slowly, and laughed at her.

He laughed, pointed a finger gun at her, pulled the trigger, and then sped off.

Mom packed overnight bags for me and Chayla and

dropped us off at my uncle Paul's and his wife Arienne's house. She took my cellphone and told me we weren't allowed to speak with Frank under any circumstances. She stayed home with Orleane.

My mom went into the bedroom and Orleane was lying on the bed. Mom stared at Orleane, tears in her eyes. "My girl, I know... and it's okay. I know." She spoke through tears.

That's when Orleane broke down and told my mom everything.

MATOTISIW is when she is having a sweat bath, but first you must dip your toes into the scalding liquid and everything inside tells you that you shouldn't do this because it is burning you, but there is also something simultaneously relieving about it.

My mom tells me I have the power of persuasion, and I think deep down she almost regrets teaching me how to effectively build an argument in favour of my point because in the most heightened moment of our lives, my persuasion prevailed.

When Chayla and I were waiting for her at my uncle's place, I begged my mom to let me visit my best friend, Alisha. My mom let me go to Alisha's under the condition that I would not leave her house. Alisha's mom picked me up and my mom informed her I was not allowed to speak with Frank under any circumstances.

Alisha is my only friend to this day who knows what my life was before. She is the only friend who has met

Frank. The only friend who knew the previous version of me, the one who had a father. I met her in grade three and we became instant best friends on the schoolyard at St. Matthews after I had just transferred in.

It was already the fifth school I had attended.

Alisha has dark skin and hair like me but the most powerful eyes. Sometimes they're green that fades into blue with a yellow centre, and other times they're more blue that fades to green in the centre. Sometimes they're soft and delicate, and other times, you should start running.

I love both sides of her.

The most beautiful thing about Alisha is her loyalty. Her love is the kind that lasts a lifetime, and she has been next to me for many lifetimes, and she will continue to be for many more. We ran away from boys together, and then chased them down and punched them in the nose. In grade four I knocked out a boy's tooth because he was bullying Alisha. His name was Adrian and I chased him down in the schoolyard. It was winter. I ran track and field and was in the running club, so it didn't take long to catch up with him. I inched closer until I was right behind him. I tackled him below the knees and sent him flying mouth-first into the layered ice on the grass. I stood up, looked down at his bleeding face, and said, "Touch Alisha again, and it'll be another tooth."

In these moments, I can really see how I was my father's daughter.

Alisha is the only person I've told every single secret. Every single one. She listens, never judges, and accepts.

She's the friend who will drive you to the house of your boyfriend you think is cheating on you to stake it out and get the proof, and then maybe help you slash his tires. We may or may not have been involved in a situation like this once, for someone else we love.

When we were in grade six, I told Alisha my secret. We were walking back to her house one day after blazing at the park with some skater boys. It was sunset and the sky was pinkish blue.

"What's up with this big secret you carry?" she said. "You know you can tell me, right?"

I thought for a moment.

It had been eating away at me; on some level, I must've known how wrong it was.

The body feels what the mind cannot process.

I was only eleven and had already been cutting myself, crying myself to sleep, sleeping with knives hidden in every corner of my bedroom.

I wouldn't even write Frank's secret in my journal, but I always spoke to Alisha of the deep dark secret that weighed on my shoulders.

My nine-, ten-, eleven-, and twelve-year-old shoulders. Four years of secrets.

We used to crush Tylenols and snort them together in her bedroom.

She watched me hurt myself, and wanted to know why.

I wanted so badly to get this off my shoulders.

To have someone I could share the burden with.

"If I tell you, you have to swear you won't tell a soul,"

I said. "I mean it. Not your mom, not a fucking soul. My dad will kill me and my life will be ruined if you do. My family will be ruined."

"I won't. I swear to fucking god." She put out her pinky.

I took it. "My dad and Orleane are in love. They're going to get married when Orleane turns eighteen."

She was quiet, but she took it all in. "I always knew there was something different between them."

She never told a soul.

That is why in this heightened moment of my life, I needed to be at Alisha's. In her room, I told her everything that had been happening. She was the only one I could speak to openly and who could understand what I was dealing with. She was the only person who knew this insurmountable, unequivocal loyalty that I felt toward Frank. I begged her to let me use her cellphone.

"I really don't think it's a good idea. Your mom said not to call him."

"I have to. I saw how many missed calls I had on my cellphone. Please, Alisha," I begged. She looked at me deeply with those green eyes and reluctantly gave me her cellphone.

"Just don't tell him where you guys are staying. I mean it, Chyana. Don't be stupid."

"I know. I won't. I just need to hear his voice."

I dialled his number that was seared into muscle memory.

After all, calling him was the motif of my childhood.

Where are you, Daddy? When are you coming home? Are you okay? Why does your voice sound like that? It's been hours. You said twelve o'clock. I'm tired of waiting. We're hungry. Where the fuck have you been? Don't you give a shit? You're always full of empty promises. Where's the weed, at least?

I loved him, still, each time he showed up.

"Dad ..." was all I could say when he answered.

"Where are you girls? What's going on? Your mom won't let me see you."

"I know. Things are fucked up."

"The cops are out looking for me. Me and your uncle Jason gotta head out of town."

He started sobbing. So did I.

"Please, tell me where you are."

"I can't, Dad. I can't." Tears streamed down my face.

"Please, Chy-Chy. I promise I won't come there. I just need to know. I won't be able to sleep if I don't."

My heart pounded and my eyes throbbed.

I gripped my chest.

The tears kept coming.

"I love you ... Chyana. Always and forever ... you will be ... my baby girl." He spoke through tears.

"I love you too, Daddy Bear."

"I promise I won't come, just please tell me where you are."

I told him.

He never came.

Sensing that his secret was about to come out, Frank and my uncle Jason and their friend ripped off their head drug dealer, hopped in a car, and fled to Ontario, without us.

When my mom picked me up at Alisha's and took me

back to Uncle Paul's, I told her that I'd called him. She told me later, when I was an adult, that she was enraged with me, but at the time, she never let it show. She never made me feel guilty for that beguiling allegiance I had to him. Not once.

The next day, we hopped in my mom's old white LeBaron and took off to a small town called Ryley in rural Alberta where her old best friend Jen now lived. Ryley was the smallest town I had ever been to, and driving along the highway lined with fields of canola, we had to laugh.

"Hahaha, do you see that grain mill over there?" I pointed out a large red grain elevator with some unexpected graffiti on it.

"Hahaha, oh my god! Does that say 'dirty shorts'?!" Orleane laughed.

We all erupted.

It was the humour we needed.

We stayed at Jen's place while my mom made a plan. This was the first weekend Orleane and I openly got drunk around my mom. I was twelve and Orleane was fifteen. I had been drinking and smoking weed for over a year already. Jen had two younger kids who were around the same age as Chayla, so they played together inside while we sat on the deck drinking vodka, shot-gunning beers, and smoking cigarettes all night long. The few nights we stayed at Jen's blended together in sadness and alcohol.

Sometimes, all you want is numbness.

While we were there my mom spoke with the police. "We're going to need the fetus," they said. "We want to test its DNA."

"I'll have to talk with Orleane. Have you found him yet?"

"They were running from the OPP, who had them surrounded in a field. Jason Logan shot himself before he was apprehended. Frank escaped. Do you know where he could've gone?"

They had a car full of drugs, guns, and money. They were pulled over at a random check stop and decided to run on foot, knowing there was no escaping prison. Frank once evaded a SWAT team by scaling the side of a building. It was all over the news when I was in grade four, and in that moment, he also somehow escaped.

My uncle Jason was separated from the other two and surrounded by cops while he was on a train track. He was breaching his parole and knew he would be locked up for a long time. In that moment, he saw death as better than captivity.

"I might be able to find out. I'll speak with my daughter and call you back."

Orleane agreed that giving the fetus to the cops was the best option for putting Frank away.

My mom is a resourceful woman. She reached out to one of my dad's sisters, my aunty Danielle. "Where are your parents living these days? I want to send them my condolences about Jason." Her heart twinged at deceiving Danielle and using her youngest brother Jason's death to do it, but her heart burned far worse for her daughter.

My aunty Danielle gave my mom the address and my mom gave it to the police the next day. "We're going to let him go to the funeral, and then we'll arrest him," they said.

"We have confirmation he's in BC. You're safe to return home."

My mom breathed a sigh of relief, but anxiety crept back in.

She called the hospital and booked the procedure for Orleane. We packed our things and headed back to the city.

The LeBaron was an old beater. I don't even know how many years my mom had that vehicle, but once, my cousin Rachel crashed it, so it had been through it. While we were driving on the highway on our way back to Edmonton, the transmission started to blow. The car slowed down from 110 kilometres per hour all the way down to fifty. And so we putt-putted along the highway, my mom terrified that we wouldn't make it in time.

PAWASKWEW is the moment when the sun filters through the clouds, always after a great storm, when the sun slices through the cumulonimbus as if their darkness hadn't covered the whole sky the moment before—it's the signal that the worst is over, but the storm is still present. The sun breaks through.

Before my mom took Orleane to the hospital, she dropped me and Chayla off at Grandma Thelma's. Grandma Thelma was a tough woman in so many ways, but she was also a guardian angel on earth. Not just for her family but for all the lives she touched, especially those of Indigenous women. Her voice was always heard. Authority and wit.

But when we arrived, my grandmother was the quietest I had ever known her to be.

She made up her bedroom for Orleane to stay in.

She had a cherry mahogany sleigh bed.

She made sure the sheets were fresh and clean.

She fluffed the pillows and made the bed as inviting as she could.

"Your sister is going to need lots of sleep," she told Chayla and me. "She needs her rest, so you just leave her alone when she gets here."

At the time, I didn't know much about what the word *abortion* meant. I didn't understand the weight of it.

I knew there was something called a fetus, and that it was no longer there.

I didn't know how my sister felt, and I never will.

I knew she was quiet, sleepy.

The house was still.

Memories.

Moments.

How can I recall certain moments with such vibrancy and then others barely at all?

I remember the feeling.

I can feel it in my chest now, but when I close my eyes, the images, the sequence of millions of rapid still frames that should be flashing, are blank.

I remember the bedroom door.

White and innocuous.

I sat outside of it, trying to listen to my sister's breaths on the other side.

The breathing sounded like sleeping.

I leaned against the door and closed my eyes.

AKOSPEYAW means the grass is wet with dew.

The day before my thirteenth birthday I stood at a podium. The judge was before me, a little to the right, and farther right still was my father in handcuffs and an orange jumpsuit.

He looked up at me, black eyes on black eyes. He sobbed. I opened my victim impact statement and read the first two sentences before I ran off the stand, crying. My aunty Debbie read the rest of it.

The judge sentenced him to four and a half years at Bowden Institution.

Four and a half years,

the quantifiable punishment for what he did.

Four and a half years,

the quantum for stealing my sister's light.

Four and a half years,

for abusing my mother for thirteen years.

Four and a half years,

for assaulting mine and my sisters' and my mother's trust and love and tossing it in the air with a grin on his lips as he pulled the trigger and blew it up into a thousand fragments.

Four and a half years,

as he watched those fragments fall and scatter slowly to the ground.

He served only two and was released on good behaviour.

He was our Witigo.

Did the spirit leave him when we placed his bones in the ground?

I used to tell people that he was a ghost.

After all, he was my burial ground.

My forgotten one.

My covered-up one.

Abandoned.

I stood above it and pointed.

It happened here.

If you start digging, you will find him.

Part II

Pinikanew

Her Bones Ache Right Through to the Marrow

WHEN I AM fourteen years old my kokum takes us to a three-day drum-making ceremony on the land. I step out of the Jeep and the smell of cedar fills my nostrils with its sweetness. There is one hour before the opening ceremony. My sisters and I wander into a corner of her acreage, tracing the paths in the forest like the lines on our palms. We crawl into a clearing filled with old wicker chairs riddled with pine needles and weathered by rain. I search for long abandoned thumbtacks in evergreen trunks—the ones I used to mark my highest climbs. I admire the ferocity of the evergreens: the one snapped in half, struck by lightning years ago, that fell in the other direction, instead of on top of our trailer. The trees are somehow smaller than the last time I stared up at them. Slightly to the right are massive boulders Frank used to build me a flower garden where I planted bluebells and alpine forget-me-nots. The flowers are now deadened stems—husks of a memory, colour merely wheat.

We are called to join the ceremony. My mother tells us to change into our long skirts before making our way to the firepit. Mother wears a ribbon skirt, and I'm wearing a blue maxi dress with a blue zip-up hoodie over top. I love the absence of vanity and the absence of hungry male eyes. I love the freedom of the forest.

The first step is in the evening and begins with the opening smudge ceremony. We stand in a circle and pray. We hold hands and only break when Elder Mae Louise stands in front of us with the smoky and sweet sage. A smudge is a cleansing and the smoke carries our prayers to the spirit world and to Creator—it can be done with sage, sweetgrass, or, my personal favourite, diamond willow fungus. It burns the slowest and smells the sweetest and is the most rare by far.

We sit in a large circle with the fire at our centre. I look around at all the women in our circle, some young, some old, all with our own wounds. Some of us know each other and some of us don't, connected by Kokum and connected forever once we leave. Our skin makes up a rainbow of tones. Some as deep as the soil, some milder like the bark on the trees, and some as pale as the moonlight, all with a lingering darkness behind our eyes—a pulsing just out of reach.

Elder Mae Louise smudges the drum, herself, and then walks around the circle until all of us have wafted the sacred sage smoke to our hands, our eyes, our mouth, our nose, our ears, down the backside of our bodies, our legs, our arms, and then, finally, to our hearts. Hiy-hiy. I press the smoke firmly to my heart and close my eyes, feeling

Creator's grace permeate my core. It radiates upward and shoots through the crown of my head, leaving a tingling sensation in its wake. When I open my eyes, Elder Mae Louise is beating the drum and she starts to sing. A song from the heart and a chant of healing. Her voice carries throughout our circle, circling around and around and around until it spirals upward, toward the spirit realm.

KÎWETINOHK KACAKASTEK means the ghosts are dancing, and when I was a little girl we used to stand in the pitch-black night on our acreage in Alberta, surrounded by evergreens reaching higher than I could climb, and watch the northern lights dance vibrantly overhead. My mother would grab me by the hand, I would grab my older sister Orleane's, and she would grab our little sister Chayla's. Frank would be somewhere near us. Maybe he walked ahead, or perhaps he followed after.

I don't remember the first time I saw the northern lights, the brilliant aurora borealis, but we always treated them as a gift. I suppose I've been watching them since I was a baby, before words took shape in my mouth. The time when my eyes were learning about this world, unadulterated by the careful curation of words—the time when what I understood was right in front of me—colours, shapes, voices, the cries of thunder, and the ticking seconds that follow the lightning awaiting the rondo of the storm.

In the dead of winter in Northern Alberta, the lights danced the loudest. In the frosted nighttime they were a symphony for those who took notice. There are no formal invitations, no playbills handed out, but it is the most exclusive display. You have to be in the right place at the right time, and only *they* choose when and for whom they will perform.

It is a common belief of my people that the northern lights are the ancestors dancing. Sometimes they dance and want you to chase—moving your feet to their guidance. Other times, they dance you all the way home.

One of my favourite stories that I used to hear sitting around the ceremonial fires is the one about a woman and the round dance.

Many moons ago, there lived a beautiful woman in the Northern Plains. This woman loved her mother deeply, more sacredly than a child had ever loved their mother. So much so that she refused to marry and instead chose to live her days by her mother's side.

The woman stayed with her mother for many, many, many years, and finally, she could feel that her mother was nearing the end of her life. She was heart-stricken. She couldn't possibly imagine how she would be able to keep living without her mother. She held on to this grief and lived out the rest of her mother's days by her side until she passed into the spirit world. The woman's worst nightmare had come true.

After the woman lost her mother, she wandered the human realm, debilitated by her loss. She wallowed in sorrow and wandered the Northern Plains day and night to cope with the physical pain of her broken heart. In the midst of her wanderings, she was taken aback to see a swirling of bright lights circling the top of a lone hill in the dead of night.

In the middle of the circle stood a figure. The woman grew curious and was instinctively drawn toward the shape, edging closer and closer until she recognized her mother. As she moved closer, she realized her mother's feet hovered above the ground.

Her mother told the beautiful daughter that she could not touch her. "I cannot find peace in the spirit world so long as you grieve for me," she said.

The daughter looked within herself and couldn't think of a way to alleviate the loss of her mother.

Her mother smiled, and spoke again. "I bring you something from the other world that will help you and everyone else in the human world grieve the loss of their deceased loved ones."

She taught her daughter the ceremony of the round dance and the songs to go with it. Together they danced the round dance on top of the hill while the ancestors joined in around them, swirling in vibrant shades of green, yellow, and red.

After the mother and daughter finished their round dance on top of the hill in the plains, the mother told her daughter: "Tell our relatives that when this circle is made, it connects us to the ancestors who will be dancing with us. In this circle, we will be one."

After the ceremony, the beautiful woman felt lighter. She looked up to the northern lights and saw her grief dancing and wisping away above her. She took this lesson back to the people to teach them the healing ceremony of the round dance.

This story of the beautiful woman who carries her grief with her while wandering the plains with a broken heart reminds me of my mother as a young woman, navigating, reaching, searching for something, someone to alleviate the loss of her own mother.

She longed to be cradled,
to feel the immense,
unwavering,
unfaltering love of a mother.

MUTWĀCHIWUN is when the water makes a noise—it murmurs, it gurgles, it purls, and at twenty-six, when I sat with my mother on my bed in my bachelor apartment, it murmured.

I was in the final semester of my undergraduate degree and had finally started writing my story. Our story. We sat cross-legged on my bed covered in soft grey and pink blankets as we started the unravelling. We were cozy—sitting across from one another like we had thousands of times before. I realized that so many of our conversations have happened in small bedrooms on comfy beds.

Almost as often as along the trails that line the river valley. We have walked those valleys hundreds of times, watched eagles, and been visited by pelicans. We sat in the rain while watching the water rush down through the bends in the riverbed, both instinctively taking off our shoes and socks and grounding ourselves in the wet soil.

That day in my apartment, the river was frozen thick and the trees in our valley were skeleton bones with frosted edges. So we sat in the comfort of my bed, with walls on all sides, nestling into the safe space we needed to create.

Our space for openness and understanding.

I began the interview with my favourite question: "What is your earliest memory?"

My mother recalled a memory of sleeping on a couch, or the floor: small limbs curled into a small ball on an area rug in a living room. Arms scooping her up and bringing her downstairs, laying her down on a sheetless mattress. She shivered. "It was always cold down there." Why did they bring her down there? She preferred the carpet. Bristles against flushed cheeks were better than stained, cold mattresses. She closed her eyes and willed herself to sleep:

She comes to me in my dreams.

It's where I get to see her.

It's where she wraps her arms around me and caresses my head.

She's always whispering something in my ears,
but I can never make it out.
Perhaps if I keep sleeping,
she will keep coming,
allowing me to get closer and closer
to hear what she is trying to say.

She woke up, cold again, and listened for footsteps above.

It was quiet.

My mother said, "Wait, I lied. There is a memory before this. One that is like a dream." Her true first memory.

She was four years old. Kokum Thelma took her to a new school for kindergarten. She heard her pull the teacher aside and say that her mother, Orleane, was dead.

I ran through the playground,
as if other little girls were chasing me,
allowing me to feel free with the wind,
but I looked back at empty air,
remembering,
it was all in my imagination.

It was a lonely feeling, but her lonely life began much earlier than that.

The rupture of familial connection, the loneliness my mother felt, began generations prior. Grandma Orleane was taken as a baby and put into residential school.

My mother has always revered her mother, but even when she was alive, she wasn't always around. She was only seventeen when she had my mom, and was often out drinking and partying with the biker gangs. Addiction is the symptom, trauma is the cause, and the repercussions are cyclical. My mother spent a couple months here and there with different family members during the formative years of her childhood. She was a roaming child with no constant love, no stability, no consistency. Motherless, even when her mother was still alive.

Uncle Bob shared that when my mother was only three years old, two years prior to her own mother dying, she hopped on an airplane to live with him and his wife and children. "You barely spoke a word, Les," he said. "It was almost like you had no emotions, which was so odd for such a small child. But when the plane took off, you clung onto my leg for the whole flight."

Eventually, my grandmother Orleane took my mother back, but at the same time she started to get her life together, she was diagnosed with cancer. She was only twenty years old.

There's a lot of speculation and filling in the gaps of my mother's childhood. She recalled times when Grandma Thelma was still drinking. She remembered waking up to go to school alone because Grandma would be sleeping. She remembers not having anything to eat, and having to make her own lunch.

"For some reason we always had plain rice cakes, haha." My mother's laughter felt important, indicative of the ways we laugh through pain to alleviate it.

Laughter is medicine.

"So that's what I would take for lunch. Felt super lonely at that time. Well, actually, that's just the theme of my life. Loneliness."

When my mom was in grade five, they moved to Edmonton from Slave Lake and Grandma Thelma started a new job with Métis Urban Housing, a low-income housing corporation for Indigenous families. Life improved during this time. My mother felt happier during this period and speculated that perhaps it was because Grandma Thelma had enough time away from her own traumas, now separated from her abusive ex-husband, Bill, and no longer self-soothing with alcohol.

"Do you remember feeling comfortable when you were living with Grandma and everyone, all of Bill's kids?" I asked. "Or looking back at your childhood, was there ever a place where you felt really comfortable?"

She never did feel that safety—that comfort that someone should feel in their own home, not until they moved to Edmonton.

In this new home, my mother faked being sick a lot. "I think that was how I was processing all the traumas of my early years. I'd stay home, watch TV on the couch. Once again, just all by myself. That's probably why I'm so used to processing my emotions by myself. When you suggested we could decompress together after doing the interview, that was mind-blowing to me. 'Cause I've always had to do the heavy emotional stuff by myself."

My mother wanted to know who her dad was, but Grandma Thelma didn't want to tell her. When Grandma Orleane was dying of cancer at twenty-one, she didn't want my mother to be raised by his wife, who was a Jehovah's Witness. Grandma Orleane didn't want her daughter to be raised in the kind of extreme religious practices that she had been forced to learn and adopt in residential school. But my mother wouldn't let it go; she wanted to speak to the man who gave her half her life.

The first memory she has of her dad, Glen, was a phone call. She begged Grandma Thelma to let her call him. She was nervous as she held the phone in her hands. She pulled its long cord and took it around the stairs, sitting on a step as her heart pounded with each ring. The phone rang and rang and rang and her breaths quickened.

He answered with his usual half yell, "Hello!"

"Hi, Dad!"

"Who's this?"

Silence. Her heart sank.

She thought, *Well, how many other daughters does he have?*

Even though it took many years for my mother to form a bond with her father, his mother was always a prominent figure in her life. Her name was Alice, but everyone called her Chickadee. She was a small but spry Cree woman who took no shit, built from bannock and blueberries. She picked blueberries faster than anyone I've ever seen and taught me about the native plants in Northern Alberta and which leaves to use for the best teas. We looked into bear shit, riddled with undigested blueberries, and determined how close the bear must be. She was a caregiver, and you knew she loved you by the pails of blueberries she would pick for you each season.

Grandma Chickadee used to clean Grandma Thelma's house for extra money, and they developed a close bond. She always sent gifts for my mother, and then for us girls. As a little girl, my mother used to have lice constantly and she would love going to Grandma Chickadee's, sitting there for hours with her picking the lice out of her head, this simple act a tender, enjoyable moment for her because she never received much physical contact as a child. Grandma

Thelma wasn't a soft woman, and definitely not the kind of woman to dole out physical affection. Grandma Thelma wasn't raised with tender affection, and so in turn, it wasn't the way she raised children, even though my mother slept in the same bed as her until she was in grade seven. The same way my mother slept with my little sister until she was in grade seven.

I remember the times I had lice as a child. I would sit on the floor in front of the couch while my mother sat behind me, combing through sections of my hair. She would pick out the eggs and place them on top of a soup can and I would crush them with my fingernails. The way the small eggs would crunch under my nail with a satisfying pop provided me with a strange joy, as if my mother and I were a team: she the hunter and me the killer, delivering the final blow to these unwelcome intruders upon my scalp.

Grandma Chickadee spent time in the Grouard residential school, but she never spoke about what happened to her there.

When the government started digging up graves at school sites, Grandma Chickadee was one of the survivors who knew where they had buried the children. In March 2022, 169 unmarked graves were found of children who had died at the Grouard residential school.

Daniela Germano reported on it for the CBC and spoke about a survivor named Rita Evans who attended Grouard for four years. She told the Truth and Reconciliation Commission that in all those years, there was little classroom instruction but mostly religious teaching and drudge work. "We were forever praying and not learning anything," Rita said, "and when I came out of grade six, my goodness, I didn't know nothing, you know, except work, work."

Another survivor from Grouard, Frank Tomkins, testified that they once made a young boy eat his own excrement because he couldn't control his bowels.

At the end of her life, Grandma Chickadee had lost some of her teeth and had short salt-and-pepper hair, but she had the softest skin with barely a wrinkle. That is how I remember her. After she lost her husband, the man she spent her entire life with, she developed Alzheimer's and dementia. It was almost as if taking care of her husband had kept her alert, and after he left this world, her soul was ready to start letting go too.

She kept telling her son, "I wanna go home to Cecil." And that's exactly what she did.

Even though her father wasn't always a consistent presence in my mother's life, Grandma Chickadee was. Glen would visit Mom once a year and spend a lot of money on her. But each summer, my mom would live with Kokum Chickadee up in Northern Alberta, and it was there that she started spending more time with her dad, building the close relationship they share today.

"So when did you end up living with Grandpa Glen," I asked my mother.

"For three months when I was in grade ten. I was getting into shit. 'Cause I started hanging around gangs and we were causing trouble in the community. Stealing cars, drinking, smoking weed, and just causing havoc in the streets, you know?"

"Was this in Slave Lake?"

"No, this was in Edmonton. So Grandma was like, 'I can't handle this, you're going to your dad's.'"

"And how come you only lived with him for three months?"

"Because it was so lonely. I was in that big house all by myself, all the time. And it didn't look like it does now—it was ... stark. He had divorced his wife and was living as a bachelor. He was always working, so he'd give me twenty bucks a day. He didn't know what to do with me. I don't fault him—all of a sudden he's got a little teenager on his hands. I was fifteen at the time."

"And you went to school when you stayed in Slave Lake? What was that like?"

"It was awful. 'Cause here I am, this big-city girl, and that's when rap music first came out and I was all into it. My hair was big. I wore the Adidas sweatshirts, with the baggy pants and the slouch socks, and listened to rap. Then I moved to Slave Lake, where all the girls had feathered hair and listened to heavy metal. So I was like this complete li'l anomaly, moving into this small town, and all the girls hated me. One of the girls, who I thought was my friend, she was like, 'All the boys only like you because your dad's rich and you're pretty.' And I'm like, 'Yeah, so?'"

We laughed.

"And then I got a note saying she wanted to fight me after school. I'd never fought before, but I met her in the forest behind the school and fought her, haha. Fist fight."

"What was that like?"

"That was really lonely too, because everyone was cheering for her. So you just realize, you're just by yourself."

"And so who won?"

"I won. It was kind of mean because she had braces, so I made sure I punched her in the mouth all the time. She didn't come to school for like a week because her mouth was all cut up."

"Brutal. But she came at you!"

"She came at me!"

My mom was new, and didn't know who to fear or who to avoid. She fell in love with running and each gym class would leave everyone in the dust. Once, she was so quick she made it back to the showers before everyone else. All the girls used to put their towels on a shower to save it, but my mom took one off and hopped in. There was a white girl in the school who everyone was afraid of, and she came and ripped the curtain open.

"That's my shower!" she yelled.

"Well, you weren't here, you fucking pervert!" my mom retorted.

Later that day, the girl tried to fight my mom in the halls, but it got broken up right away.

"So, yeah, it was just super lonely. At school, at home with Dad because he was never there, and it was winter, so it was dark all the time... I came back home to Edmonton for Christmas and never went back. I just cried to Grandma, 'I don't wanna go back there.' So she let me stay. But I started hanging around again with the same people, and that's when I met Darcy."

My mother had not yet sung the songs of the round dance. Her grief had not yet danced up and out of her and into the aurora borealis. The northern lights had not yet carried it away.

My mom longed for arms to hold her and never let go.

Eventually, she found them.

THE SECOND STEP of the drum-making ceremony is cutting the hide. Many skins lie on the grass and we examine them, touch them, look for imperfections that will work with the shape of our drums. We plunge the skins into water and soak them overnight. The water must be cold; otherwise, it will break the skins down too much, rendering them unusable. A nearby lake will work well. The pond dried up years ago, so instead we use basins. I let my fingers linger in the water with the hide until I feel a slimy sensation. We sit around the fire and tell stories and share teachings. The flames crackle.

OOCHISTIN is when it leaks, but it only refers to the idea of water coming into and not out of something—at this moment, the fissure had begun, until, eventually, it overflowed.

The first man my mother ever loved had a big family. There were always people running around the house and voices she could hear through the walls. His name was Darcy. He had long, silky, bone-straight hair dark as night. His black eyes twinkled when he laughed, radiating energy and charisma. He was always the focus of the room, people naturally gravitating toward his orbit as he cracked jokes.

In those days the neighbourhood hall threw dance parties for teenagers.

My mother begged her uncles to take her. "Please, I'm finally fifteen. Literally a teenager. Can I please go?" Her uncles were more like big brothers because they were all raised in the same household. They were the big badasses of the neighbourhood—the gang-affiliated tough guys.

"Fine, we'll chaperone you at the dance," Uncle Bob gave in. "Go get ready!"

When they arrived, she went off to dance with some of her friends. It was the eighties, so rap music was just emerging and all the girls had big hair and leather jackets. This tough girl from the neighbourhood who hung out with all the gang guys pulled my mom aside.

"Look, you know my buddy Darcy, right? Well, he wants to dance with you."

"Thanks, but I'm not interested."

"I'll tell you what, if you go with him, then I'll be your protection and make sure no one fucks with you."

Other girls were always trying to fight my mom because she was the new girl in the city, and pretty. This could be exactly what she needed. "Fine," she said.

She didn't know that one dance would begin to shape her whole life. Hanging out with Darcy and his crew was like being part of a community, something she had always longed for. Soon enough, they were together constantly. She started drinking, smoking pot, breaking and entering. One day, she finally went home after sleeping at Darcy's place for a few nights.

"You think I don't know what you're up to out there?" Grandma Thelma demanded.

"What do you mean—"

Grandma Thelma punched her square in the nose and told her to get the fuck out. My mom took off and went to the mall, hoping Grandma Thelma would calm down. She and her best friend, Charm, met up with some neighbourhood kids, smoked some pot, and then she went home.

She didn't find a softened heart welcoming her back. Instead, she found her stuff in garbage bags on the front porch. She had nowhere to go. She wandered the streets for a while, before she wound up at Darcy's and moved in with his family. It was the closest place she had to a home.

One day, Darcy locked her in the bedroom and told her she couldn't leave. She tried to escape out the window, but he chased her down in the yard and threw her back inside.

She romanticized his abuse as passion and equated it with love.

She always knew her relationship was a little fucked up, but isn't that what they were supposed to be like?

That was love, wasn't it?

That was passion.

Fists being thrown and bodies being shoved. When she was six or seven years old, she came home from school one day to find Bill beating Grandma Thelma in the front yard.

She ran up to them and started hitting his leg, telling him, "You leave my grandma alone!"

So when Darcy hit her she didn't think much about it. This was just what happened when two people were in love. She could handle the odd punch or two, and she'd give it right back. But don't disrespect her by cheating on her. That was a different ball game.

When she was sixteen, she got pregnant with my older sister, Orleane.

When she was six months pregnant, she caught Darcy cheating on her. She woke up in the middle of the night and he wasn't in bed. She snuck out of the room and tip-toed downstairs. There he was. On the couch fucking one of his cousin's friends. She threw punches instinctively until he shouted, "Les, you're pregnant! What the fuck are you doing?!" The next day she packed her shit and left.

She was seventeen years old, the same age her own mother had been when she had her.

When my sister Orleane was one, she and my mom lived in a house with Charm. My mom was eighteen and had just received her trust fund from the reserve. Charm had this cousin—known as Frankie—who called her all the time from prison. One day Charm wasn't home, so my mom answered the phone. He was lonely, so she talked with him instead.

He was charming and charismatic, and my mother was not a woman you can ignore. She smiles and hearts are seized. She is the kind of woman who walks through the woods in bare feet and does not wince when thorns prick blood from her soles. She hunts for western red cedars, and when she meets one she stares up at it from a bed of moss. She does not cower in the face of giants. She will walk right up to that red cedar and wrap her arms around it, allowing its energy to flow through her, as she allows her own to pass through it.

My father had a powerful voice that commanded ears to open. He courted her over the phone, talked about dates they would go on, places they would see. He talked about the saltwater shores in Vancouver. He wrote her letters and poems, made her jewellery.

My mom fell in love with a broken, incarcerated man. When he got out of prison, they began their lives together.

He treated Orleane like his own daughter, and together they built a family.

When they moved to the West Coast, my mom saw salt water for the first time. She let the salty air blow through her hair, bouncing through her ringlet curls. The three of them sat on the beach and searched for starfish on the rocky shore.

"I looked at the two of them together, so happy that I had found a father for my beautiful little girl." When my mother spoke these words, I could see the pain in her eyes bubbling up and threatening to fall. "So happy that I had found myself a person who professed his love for me from his core." Her stomach shook as she wiped the tears away.

Like Darcy, Frankie had a personality that lit up a room, and then he could take that light away in a breath.

Both their personalities possessed a kind of gravity that is hard to move away from, hard to not move toward. Frank's laughter was loud, charged, and usually followed with a *maaaaah.* But his anger—his anger was unbridled and immobilizing. While his laughter evoked smiles and eruptions of laughter from bellies, his anger expelled all happiness from the room.

Frank didn't show Mom his dark side right away. Maybe it was calculated, but maybe there are parts of bad people that are still good. Perhaps we are all good people but with great capabilities for harm.

When my mother met Frank's father, Frank Sr., she saw where Frankie had inherited his terrifying moods. Frank Sr. was a survivor of the Sixties Scoop and the school of hard knocks. When my dad was a little kid, he watched his dad raise clenched fists to his mother with a bottle never far from his lips. As children, he and my uncle Jason also suffered underneath those unbridled fists. "That fucked Frankie up," my mom recalled, "being the oldest of his brothers and trying to protect them but failing miserably." From a young age, he inherited that violence, landing himself in and out of the prison system for his whole life.

Frank's violent episodes always resulted in him threatening his own suicide. When my mom was pregnant with me, he held a gun to her head and threatened to kill her. She begged him for her life before he allowed salt water to pour from his eyes, and then turned the gun toward himself. Now she was pleading for his life instead of her own.

My father apologized to my mother, sobbing, before pulling her into an embrace. "I love you, Les."

She felt immense relief.

"I got to keep my family."

The first time my mother shared this story with me, an alternate reality flashed before my eyes. A reality that has plagued many stories, many people. A man killing his children, then killing his wife, and then killing himself. Why is it that people come to harm those closest to them? Where is the rupture? Is it innate? In the brain? Society? Someplace deeper?

There is a very close reality in which I would never have been. And if my parents had never met, the lack of my existence would also be true. Yet I was born to the spirits of the salt.

Born amid the threat of violence, tears in the eye,
but also amid great love,
dew on the skin
shared between two bodies in love.

Three years later, my little sister joined us on the salty shores.

Together, they built me and Chayla.

My mom's very own family.

Her very own cradling love.

But Frank could never keep a job for longer than a few months. He would be doing well, making decent money, and then one day my mom would come home to find him sitting on the couch, playing video games. "A couple of days would go by of him doing nothing, and then he would pawn everything we owned to make ends meet. Eventually, when we were almost homeless, he would find another job, and we'd have to rebuild. That was our cycle," she concluded.

Once a year his fists would pour, and then he would be petals, and they would do it all over again. For thirteen years their friends and family thought my mother was just a clumsy woman.

"Thirteen years," she said. "Thirteen years I lived that life with him."

Sitting on my bed together, she told me how proud she was of me, about to graduate university, finally writing my book, her old soul of a daughter.

Her spirit of the salt.

We reminisced about the time when I was a kid and jumped out the trailer window, butt naked.

"I saw you running around outside naked," she said. "I distracted your da—Frankie, so he wouldn't see."

I never knew all the little ways she would try to keep us safe. In a way, she is like the Pakakos, the skeleton spectre who soars above the forest, preying on disrespectful hunters who kill unnecessarily. She hunted my father, the Witigo who preyed on his own family. The Plains Cree woman's silent attack in the night took down the sorcery of the Woodland Cree Witigo.

THE THIRD STEP of the drum-making ceremony is when the sun rises and we begin with the smudge. Elder Mae Louise wafts the sacred smoke over each child of Creator.

We share stories, take turns speaking about what brought us here. I hold the talking drumstick, but I know I am too young and too hungover to speak about locked bedrooms, broken walls, and my father in an orange jumpsuit. Instead, I share what I hope to learn. Others share what they want to release, or sometimes, we say nothing at all. Silence with tears. Silence with heaviness. Silence with acceptance. Sometimes the greatest power lies in the things that remain unsaid. When they are ready they will be spoken, or even written; written is okay too.

KUSKĀWĀO is when she passes from one piece of water to another, and after Métis Urban Housing found us a new placement, we moved to a predominantly white neighbourhood on the south side of Edmonton.

I went to Kenilworth junior high and was surrounded by guiltless faces that carried crayons and neatly bow-tied childhoods—my face carried demons and Band-Aids. I came from a neighbourhood where we bought weed from men who stood outside corner stores and stole liquor from our parents and dizzied ourselves in parks with limbs too small to bear all that we'd endured. When I walked into that new school and stared at those young, white faces, all I saw was a reflection of everything I never had. They were kids who didn't worry about where their next meal would come from or how much a pair of pants cost. We were kids having a shopping spree in Walmart because welfare accidently gave us an $800 gift card instead of an $80 one.

I hated them in their pastel-coloured shorts and neatly side-swept bangs.

They wore smiles that reeked of unadulterated ignorance.

I longed for that bliss.

While I was at that school, it felt like no adults there wanted me to succeed, with the exception of the principal, Mr. Skoreyko.

I was sitting in math class, bantering with another student when he said, "At least my dad isn't a pedophile."

My heart sank and a swell of anger took control of my body. It had only been a few months since I'd helped put my father in prison for what he did.

There was a rage inside me that I hadn't yet learned how to release or control. I was banned from wrestling class because of the time we'd been playing queen of the mat and it came down to me and one girl. She did something that hurt me and I blacked out. When I came to, I was throttling her, hands wrapped around her throat, pinning her to the mat. The teacher ripped me off her and I had to apologize to the girl and her whole family.

When this kid said what he said about my father, I felt my temper slipping away. My best friend, Alisha, had convinced her mom to let her switch schools to be with me, and she was sitting next to me. She grabbed my hand and pulled me out of the classroom. "Fuck that kid, Chyana. He's not worth it."

We walked to my locker and I opened it, breathing in and out, in and out. I searched my locker until my hands settled on a Vera Wang perfume bottle. I wrapped my palm around its thick, heart-shaped glass. "I'm going to smash this on his fucking head."

"Give me that right now! Don't you fucking dare!" Alisha yanked the perfume from my hands right as the bell rang and I watched that kid stroll out of class, striding lankily to his locker, oblivious of the harm he had caused me.

Hands now empty, I paced over to him, ripped the glasses from his face, and stomped on them, over and over and over and over until they crumbled into a million little fragments. I swivelled on my heel quicker than he could even react and marched to the principal's office, blowing past the receptionists, who were yelling after me, "Chyana, what do you think you're doing?! You can't go back there!" I flipped them off and screamed, "Fuck you!" through tears and barged straight into Mr. Skoreyko's office. I sat on the chair in front of his desk and started sobbing.

"Chyana, what's going on?" he asked.

I broke down and told him everything. The courtroom. My father. Frank. The things I used to see. The anger. The hurt. All while heaving uncontrollably across from him.

He listened, passed me tissues, and said, "I understand."

The other kid was suspended, and from that moment, I knew Mr. Skoreyko was someone I could actually count on.

THE FOURTH STEP of the drum-making ceremony is when we break from the circle and find our stations, which hold hides and a round birch wood frame. Birch is malleable. We are malleable too. It's time to build. We lay the hide flat, feeling its slippery slickness. We lay the birch frame on top and stretch the hide to make sure it folds up and over the edges, leaving enough room to punch holes for lacing and weaving. There can't be too much slack, but there must also be enough, because once the hide dries it will tighten to the frame, giving the drum its voice and vibration. If it's too loose, its voice will not carry. If it's too tight, the strings will snap and the drum will not sing.

PÚKOOPÃO is when she goes into the water, and for the first time I knew that I had to submerge myself in a different kind of water—cleansing water to release everything my body had endured and stored and held for the first sixteen years of my life.

After we moved to the south side of Edmonton, Orleane and I stopped hanging out with certain cousins on my mom's side of the family. We realized the only thing that really kept us together was drinking and drugs. It all culminated on a night when Marcus punched Orleane out cold, and then knocked me out when I stood up for her. He was one of our cousin's best friends, one of *our* good friends. All I remember is waking up in a puddle of my own blood, and I had a popped blood vessel in my eye with dark bruises to match for weeks afterward. My cousins sat on the couch and didn't do a single thing.

I believe they're still friends with Marcus to this day.

Grandma Thelma often organized events for what felt like family, even though many women I wasn't related to were there. She could see how broken we all were and wanted to help us through it—she saw how out of touch with the rest of the family we had become. We had become our own island because it was the only way my mother knew how to protect us.

My grandma always brought us together, though. She was a matriarch incarnate and brought one of the most profound moments of my life into existence. She weaved it, and I know she weaved those moments for so many people over her years.

Grandma Thelma organized a weekend-long women's retreat at Elder Joyce Beaver's house in Sandy Lake for the most powerful healing ceremony I have ever participated in.

That weekend, the sun pierced the clouds overhead, but it wasn't overpowering. We slept in a teepee with a fire in the middle, warming us through the chill spring nights. Standing in one place, I turned slowly until I spun myself dizzy, nothing but trees and bush and greenery blurring together in a haze. Long birch branches were laid out in rows on the moss-covered earth. We wandered through the woods, searching for round stones that would break your toes if you dropped them. One by one, I carried them into the fire, heating them up and respecting their strength and durability.

Respecting their defiance of defeat.

My family met an Indigenous Elder named Lorraine. My sisters, my mother, and I all felt like we had met her before. It was like meeting family.

She told us that we would all be seeing each other again, and she was right.

All of us women wandered out into the forest in search of bones of the earth. We gathered birch branches and shaped them into a dome and placed blankets and hides on top, building a womb from the dirt and allowing Mother Earth to cradle us. One by one, we carried the scalding rocks from the fire into the pit in the centre of the dome, and once they were all in, us women followed after and blanketed the entry with a hide.

Cedar branches dipped in water graced with berries and sage splash the faint glow from the rocks, filling the womb with steam and sweet sticky scents. The Elder starts the first of four rounds and soon the pitch black is filled with song and heat and we all begin to pray to Creator. The first set of songs reverberates through the darkness, cradling the anguished souls who relinquished themselves into Creator's healing grace. The saltwater droplets that pour from my eyes meet the spirits of the steam and together they meld in a perfect dance that honours Mother Earth. The second set of songs slashes through my core as we sing for the sisters, the mothers, the women of the earth. I find my weeping mixing with the power of the voice that bellows out into our cradling cavern as I break down for the healing of my mother and sisters in the physical realm, and then my ancestors. My body shakes as I feel the vibration from Mother Earth creeping up into my bones as she spreads her warmth within me. I radiate that warmth as I spread it outward further still with all women in my thoughts and heart, all the incarcerated sisters, all the murdered sisters, all the broken and lost sisters. I pray for their healing and grace, and for their power to return to them. The power of Indian women can never be taken away, only hidden. I allow the feelings to overpower me as I stare straight ahead in the darkness, a dancing of colours and auras before me. I greet my grandmother Orleane for the first time and I know I won't see her again until my soul leaves this body and enters the spirit world once again. I allow the tears to stop as I see her vibrant white light, knowing she is sending me her guidance and strength, knowing she is telling me that she is here with all of us, protecting us. The third round is the hardest because we pray for the brothers. The third round is the one where I weep the most because I allow myself to pray for my perpetrator and his healing. I weep the most because I am finally able to weep for my uncle Jason, who took his own life, and I pray for his soul and I allow myself to mourn for him for the first time. I feel his soul and he forgives me for not crying when he passed. He forgives me for not going to his funeral. He tells me he knows why. His soul hugs me as he allows me to release those emotions, and at the end of this round, I am free. The fourth round comes and the songs fill my belly and I am lighter, but then a wall slams into me as I begin to pray for myself, a damaged and broken sister along with the others, praying for my healing and my power to come back to me. I open my wounds and allow the mixture of my salt and the spirits of the steam to fold their way into every crevice of my body that is leaking blood and drugs and alcohol. When I open these wounds it is different from the times I dragged a blade into my earth-stained skin. When I open these wounds it isn't to numb the gut-clenching pain that seizes my insides. When I open these wounds it is to allow the love and light and healing to infiltrate every crevice. It is not a Band-Aid opening; it is the elixir opening. As this round comes to an end, I feel the mud from Mother Earth covering my wounds, and when I exit her womb, the air assaults my drenched skin and the mud falls away, leaving my cedar skin fresh with new bark.

Nohkôm Thelma, who had stayed in the house, told me: "While you sang, four eagles soared above you in a circle."

THE FIFTH STEP of the drum-making ceremony is time to punch the holes. We fold the hide circle in half and fold and punch, fold and punch, fold and punch, until sixteen sets of holes roll around the perimeter. I run my fingers along the top of the wet and slippery skin that belongs to a deer. I bring my nose up close and take a deep breath. I like the way it feels under my skin. It's gentle and I am gentle and in this moment I weep. I weep to give thanks and I weep to ensure that my tears are built with my drum and the tears of the deer. If deer cry, I hope the tears live in their skin the way mine do.

KIMEWUNISKAKOO is when it rains upon her, and sometimes when the rain beats down upon you long and hard enough, you begin to absorb it to the point where the only thing left to happen is condensation, and the liquid begins to pull from within you; for me, I pulled it out of me and created storm clouds within bottles.

At the beginning of grade eleven, I was expelled from McNally High School. The school constable caught me smoking a joint outside the school on a day when I had just picked up an ounce of mushrooms and an ounce of weed in preparation for the weekend ahead. The authorities suspected I had been selling drugs to other students and they weren't wrong. I still hadn't turned sixteen, so the school board committee legally declared me sixteen in the court of law so they could expel me.

I sat in a dimly lit boardroom, across from white faces staring down at the delinquent little brown girl—that's what I was: a fifteen-year-old little girl who needed people to see her and want her to succeed, but those people wanted me to stop "corrupting" their precious white children and get out of their school. So I was expelled from the only place that was giving me any sense of routine. Across the table sat Ms. Long, the vice-principal who loathed me, staring at me with a smug smile on her pinched face.

After that, it was a slow but steady decline. My drinking accelerated, and drug use followed. I was so promiscuous that I couldn't even recall what had happened to me or my body, and the way I dealt with that was more drugs, more drinking, more numbing myself. I hid how miserable I was and played the part of the happy party girl who wanted everyone, including myself, to have a good time. I always had a smile on my face and it was my mission to bring the same to those around me.

Each day a horizontal flip-sided crescent moon rested upon the skin covering the bones of my face. Each morning it rose with the sun, my personal ecliptic greeting to any face that encountered mine. I knew I had succeeded if periodically throughout the day those faces staring back at me bared their teeth, flipped their moons, tilted back their heads, and allowed noise to escape their red lips. Job well done. I made them happy. I made them smile. I made them laugh. If the people around you were happier, then surely you would be too, right?

Sunshine chasing moon; that is what I had always done.

I kept myself busy. I was never home. I filled my time constantly with people and substances because those moments when I did find myself alone were unbearable. I had been running from Frank and all our memories for the last five years—longer. All the years I held on to his secret. All the years I had to watch him harm my sister. All the years he harmed all of us. I hated myself. I hated the things I had done. I hated that I loved him. I didn't feel worthy of anything. I disgusted myself and would cry at night.

My moon was saved for the daytime; my nighttime was for the blackness.

Pitch.

Silent.

Empty.

Abyss.

Abysmal.

My nighttime was abysmal.

No sun, no stars, no moon. Just me and the dark corridors of my mind.

After I was expelled, my mom told me she was sending me away to live with our Elder Lorraine to get clean. I kicked and screamed and cried and told her that if she tried, I would move out and never speak to her again.

Then Orleane got an offer to spend three months in Africa with our uncle and his wife. The thought of being away from her for three months was a huge part of why I eventually gave in to my mother. I wanted Orleane to go away. Not because I wanted to be away from her, but because I wanted, more than anything, for her to heal. But—*What would I do without her?* We slept beside each other every night.

I didn't want to cry myself to sleep. I didn't want to keep having nightmares. I wanted to black out so that I didn't dream. I wanted to black out so that the memories wouldn't come. I quit my job and Orleane and I committed the entire month before she went away to partying every single day. It all came to a head on a night when I was sixteen, after Orleane had left.

I was dancing at a bar and got kicked out for being too drunk. I don't remember how I got home, but I crawled in through the window. The first time I heard the song "My Own Worst Enemy" by Lit it was like I was listening to a song I had written about myself, at the point in my life when it was the worst it had ever been. The lead singer begins the song by bellowing about melancholy blackouts and ends by serenading the listener with self-loathing.

Alone in my room, I slammed back shot after shot from the bottle on the table. A flash. Wandering around outside in my pyjamas. *Where am I? Why isn't anyone answering their phone? I am alone. Again. I can't feel my legs. Alone. No.*

I filled the bong and inhaled deep. *Hold it in since it's the last one.* When I exhaled there was no smoke left to blow out. I got up and poured another shot. I didn't take the chase and instead let the burn take full control of my esophagus. I saw my notebook on the table and began to write:

> *The cringe of my stomach and the throbbing of my heart is a dark and crowded room. It's a room that is filled with the tears that shed from my wilted soul. I can't breathe. Inhale, inhale, inhale. Alone. Sometimes I want to jump out of a window and see if I can fly and I won't be disappointed if I die.*

I tossed the notebook and the pen to the side. Poured another one. It burned a little less. I didn't mind the burn, though. I grabbed a cigarette and smoked it near my window, letting in the cold summer morning air. I watched the smoke as it wafted up and out. The sun began to rise.

I poured another one and realized the bottle was almost empty. I lay down on the couch across from my bed and stared at the ceiling. The menacing quiet of my room inched closer from all sides until I was in a spotlight amid a sea of silence. The pressure bore down until my eyes began to well, and soon enough they overflowed. The salty droplets fell down the sides of my head and crusted in my straightened chestnut hair.

Looking up, I saw the heat vent without a cover on it.

Where did the cover go?

Running through the centre of the vent was a metal pipe. I wonder where it came from and where it's headed. Does it remember? How the fuck did that pipe end up there? It's cold and ugly and I hate it. It's dirty and tainted and no one will ever love it because it doesn't even love itself. How could it? It's a dingy, dark, and rusted bone.

No one loves the rusted bones.

I walked to my closet.

I grabbed the belt from my bathrobe.

I hopped up onto the couch and tied the belt to that abhorrent pipe, and then I tied the other end around my neck. I breathed heavily as I stood on the back of the couch. The clutching of my heart weighed down harder and the sea of silence became louder and louder, sea-salted water leaking down my cheeks and onto my bare collarbone.

Alone. Alone. Alone. I don't want to be here anymore.

I am tired.

Daddy, I am so tired.

You were so big and strong and scary that you took my strength away.

I hate you and I hate myself.

I love you.

I jumped off the back of the couch. I felt the pull around

my neck, and then I went crashing to the floor. The pipe broke. I propped myself onto my forearms as I dry heaved on the floor.

I crumbled and collapsed,
silently sobbing onto the cold concrete floor.
I cradled myself on the floor,
the belt still fastened around my neck.

It was late in the afternoon when I woke up with my hair half-matted to the back of my head. The sun was peeking through my curtains, illuminating the coffee table covered in crusted joint roaches, the concrete floor littered with ashes. There was a two-six of gin on the table with a single shot left inside.

The night before pounded at my skull.

Alone. Alone. Alone. I don't want to know.

I went into my phone and deleted all my texts before I could read them. My chest was tight and an invisible hand gripped that delicate organ that was pumping extra hard that morning. My anxiety and shame melded and came pounding at my sanity. There is temporary leave in the blackout. I grabbed the bottle of gin, pressed it to my lips, and took the last shot. I allowed myself to feel the burn and it eased the pressure of the hand that held my weakened heart.

I set the bottle back down and the spirits of the salt assaulted my eyes.

My hands shook as I walked upstairs and into my mother's room.

While my chest heaved, I managed to say, "I'm ready… to go."

My mom wrapped her arms around me and held on tight.

I felt like a red cedar.

"Pack your things. We'll leave this week."

THE SIXTH STEP of the drum-ceremony is weaving. We grab the long strings we cut from the hide on the first night and begin. We punch a hole at the tip of the string, and then feed it through the first hole set, under and then over and through. This first weaving acts as the anchor. We centre the birch frame on the middle of the hide, and then stretch the hide up and over the edges, bringing the string across the drum, weaving the hole set across from it, and then continue the pattern in a circular motion. Up and through and over and across: braiding. Picture weaving a shoelace back and forth through the holes, and then continuing up and down until the shoe is tied. With the drum, instead of lacing it up and down, we lace it in a circular motion until all sixteen hole sets have been laced up. Then we leave the drums out to dry.

YÂWASKENAM means she can barely touch the ground in deep water, and sometimes you need something else, a new force to pull you into the shallow end.

The night before I left to stay with Elder Lorraine, I told my mom, "If I'm really going to get sober and change my life, I want to have one last chill hurrah."

"Look at everything that has happened to you already," she said. "Are you sure that's what you really want to do? Don't you think it'll just make it harder than it's already going to be?"

"It'll just be my closest friends in the backyard, so you can keep an eye on me. Just one last time."

"Fine. But we're leaving at noon tomorrow and I don't care how hungover you are."

"Yup!"

I invited my closest friends over and we drank in the backyard. We had a fire and passed around the bong. I jumped up and down on the trampoline, spinning round and round. The grass blurred with the silhouettes of people bringing bottles to their lips, and the laughter ricocheted off the garage before landing on my face. On the last jump, I pushed my legs forward and my butt bounced me up high into the air before I landed back down. I crawled to the edge of the tramp and someone handed me a bottle of vodka. I brought it to my lips and savoured the burn as I let it alter my consciousness.

My friend Shayna came up to me and we hugged drunkenly. "I can't believe you're leaving," she said.

"I know. It's so fucked up, right?"

"You were the first person I smoked weed with. I can't even picture you not smoking weed anymore! It's good, though, I'm proud of you."

"Haha, remember the first time we met?"

"You hated me, haha!"

"I remember we were in the school gym. You walked

right up to me, all tall and blonde and lanky. You were so extra. 'Hi, I'm Shayna!' waving in my face like the happiest thing I ever saw."

"Haha, you just stared at me with this straight face. Everyone knew you as this intimidating girl who walked down the hallways and never smiled."

I recalled that time, eating lunch alone in bathroom stalls: *Why is there blood on the floor? Maybe you had your period—you should check. Crack whore. Your dad's a pedophile. Vibrations. Water bottle smashed into an eyeball. You are so dead. You're the one on the floor.*

"Sometimes there's nothing to smile about," I said. "I think that's why you annoyed me so much. I couldn't understand how someone could just walk around so happy all the time. I thought you had to be fake."

"I guess we owe it all to Mr. T."

"Haha, we do!"

"Remember when he partnered us up in grade nine?"

"We never actually thanked him for that. Imagine if he didn't... We never would've become friends. I never would've found out that you are, truly, genuinely just this blonde little happy girl. That smile you wear is one of the realest things I know."

Mr. T ended up passing away before we could ever thank him for partnering us up.

"And I never would've found out the reason why you didn't smile."

"Well, cheers to knowing each other." I tapped my can of beer to hers.

"Seriously, though... you really fucking scared me that one night. I'm glad you're going to get help."

"Yeah, I'm sorry you had to see that. It was a dark night."

"I've never seen anything like that. I felt helpless. I didn't know what to do. We were so drunk and there you were... sitting in your dark fairy Halloween costume, crying and cutting yourself. I just remember crying and begging you to stop." Her eyes began to well.

"I know. Sometimes I just couldn't stop myself. It was how I learned to deal with these feelings inside."

"I think this is gonna be really good for you."

I smiled at her. "Should we go take a shot?"

She poured us each one. "Blondie and Brownie for life!"

When I woke up the next morning, the hangover wasn't as bad as it should've been. The body builds up a tolerance to whatever you throw at it.

I finished packing my bag, and my mom called down the stairs, "Chyana, are you ready?"

"Be right up!" I took one last rip from my bong, holding it in until there was no smoke left to blow out. Exhaled it anyway. Let the calm wash over me.

I trudged up the stairs, through the kitchen, and out the front door. I tossed my bag in the back of my mom's Jeep, hopped in the front seat, rolled down the window, lit a cigarette, and away we went.

I inhaled the warm air and stared out at the lilac trees that were beginning to bloom and the four tall pine trees that lined the perimeter of our duplex. The one closest to the road always looked like it was dying a little, slowly, year after year, the other three leaching its water, making it the runt of the litter.

I took it all in and wondered how I would feel when I came back.

Before long, we were on the flat, open prairie road and the wheat fields were interspersed with canola. Canola, though it looks vibrant and beautifully yellow, has a terribly pungent scent. The sky was perfectly blue, barely a cloud.

Off to Calling Lake I went.

The reserve.

Sobriety.

We pulled into the driveway of a small but sturdy white wooden home with a large yard and a porch on the side. I jumped out of the Jeep, grabbed my bag out of the back seat, and walked with my mom to the side of the house, where we found Elder Lorraine.

She hugged me. Lorraine was the same height as me, her frame a little larger, with warm, golden-brown eyes. Her hair was slightly longer than shoulder length and soil-rich brown peppered with a few greys. Her cheekbones pointed toward the sky.

I peeled away from our hug and told her, "I want to apologize beforehand, in case I'm a complete bitch while I'm here. It's been a long time since I've gone without weed and alcohol."

She laughed. "Don't worry. I've handled much worse."

We all chuckled. We went inside for tea and bannock and had a visit before it was time for my mom to hit the road again. She hugged me and kissed me on the top of my head.

"Be strong, my girl, and call anytime. I love you. You can do this."

"I know. Thank you, Mom. For bringing me here. I love you too."

I shut my tears back inside.

I was staying in Lorraine's nineteen-year-old son Raymond's room. I set my bag down on the floor next to the bed made up with fresh linens and blankets.

I never knew that I would find what I had been lacking on the reserve in Calling Lake. Lorraine's sons were the first sober friends I'd ever had and I became best friends with Raymond's cousin Chuck and we all had horror movie nights in the abandoned church. We ate snacks and laughed and rowed the boat on the lake. For the first time in my life, I was beginning to find what felt like actual happiness.

It took Raymond and me two weeks to fall in puppy love. As deep and true as love can possibly be when you're sixteen years old. We became insomniacs together, staying up until the sun glimmered on the horizon while professing to each other the stories of our lives. We cuddled on the porch under the stars and shared theories about aliens and life after death.

You remove a girl from her habits, her rituals, her vices, and you take away her defence mechanisms. There was no escaping Raymond—no hookup that I could then walk away from and not speak to again, no phone number to block, friend request to ignore, because I was living in his house, in his bedroom. I was terrified of being close, of allowing myself to be vulnerable, of allowing my heart to rest in another's palms.

I reflected on the last guy I'd had in my bed before Calling Lake and the words I'd spoken to him: "Please don't fall in love with me because you will be disappointed." I ignored his texts for weeks.

Two months later, and two days before I was going back to Edmonton, Raymond and I had sex for the first time. And the next night we got into a fight about who knows what and broke up.

It felt like love was certainly—or at least almost always—a lie.

I was still proud of myself. I quit cigarettes, weed, and alcohol. I journalled. I sat with myself. I was alone at night without my Band-Aids. I was better.

Not completely healed, but better.

THE SEVENTH STEP comes the following morning when we make the drumsticks. We pick and sand our handles, and then sew a small piece of suede into a small pocket and stuff it with cotton, attaching it to the end of the stick and tying it tight with sinew. The way we use parts of the animal to stitch it back together amazes me. Deconstructing it just to reconstruct it with the same bits it had originally, if slightly different. It reminds me that nothing can be destroyed, not entirely, or at least that things that appear destroyed can always be rebuilt or reformed or somehow evolve into something that renders the act of destruction impossible.

ASECIWAN is when the water flows backward, and I have to take a minute to think about what that means. Can the damage be undone? Is it possible for the water to truly unravel? Perhaps not. Perhaps the water flowing backward is always indicative of something having gone very wrong, but even still, perhaps we must follow the backward flow to see where it leads.

On an overcast day when I was sixteen, I had just moved back into the city from Calling Lake and enrolled in Fresh Start high school to begin my grade twelve year. I decided to go visit Mr. Skoreyko. When I arrived at Kenilworth, they told me he was now the principal at McNally High School—the school I'd been told to not step foot in again.

By the time I left Kenilworth the sun was shining and the sky was that perfect shade of September blue. I hopped on my bike and rode all the way to McNally and walked through the doors that I'd been pushed out of only a year before. I felt like a new person, but also an intruder.

When I walked into the office, I saw Ms. Long immediately—the woman who wanted me expelled more than anyone else.

"You are not allowed to be here, Chyana. What do you think you're doing?"

"I know, but I need to see Mr. Skoreyko."

"Does he know you're coming?" Her tone was scathing.

"No, he doesn't, but just tell him that Chyana is here to see him."

She turned her nose up at me as the receptionist called into his office. Within moments, he came out of his office, a wide smile beaming across his face. "Chyana! What a surprise! Please, come inside."

I strode into his mahogany office and took a seat, smiling past Ms. Long.

"So, tell me everything! What are you up to now?"

"Well, I just enrolled in Fresh Start. The 'go at your own pace' learning centre."

"No, you didn't."

I was so confused. "Um, yes, I did."

"No, you didn't. You're coming here."

"But how? I was expelled, and Ms. Long would never let me come back."

"Don't you worry about that. You just show up here in my office tomorrow morning and we'll get you enrolled in all your classes."

I was stunned. And I was happy because it meant that I could have another chance at a normal high school experience. I could have cried. I sped home to tell my mom.

That night, I prayed for the first time in a long time. I lit my sage and asked Creator to give me a sign that this was the right decision for me.

The next day I was walking to class, iced coffee in hand, feeling the brisk fall morning air of Alberta. I sauntered past a stop sign, but then quickly backed up because I noticed something perched against it. It was a licence plate that read JAN12. My birthday. A tingly sensation pulsed up and down my body and my eyes began to well. I picked up the licence plate and looked around. There was no one, not even a vehicle, in sight. I didn't know that when I asked for a sign, I would get a literal one posted against a stop sign. It was uncanny.

I placed it in my bag and still have it to this day.

Mr. Skoreyko didn't see a troubled girl who brought others down; he saw a bright kid who needed help escaping a dark past.

If it weren't for him, who knows where I would have ended up.

PUSSIPĀYOOWĀO is when the wind blows over the surface of the water, and I think of the thousands of tiny ripples that push along the surface, pirouetting a symphony moments before the rain falls—the small indication that the raindrops are about to pierce the water below.

On June 11 of that year—Frank's birthday—I put my headphones in and walked. I walked along the tree-lined sidewalks until I found my way to a bench on Strathearn Drive.

The wind gusted through my dark brown hair, picked up my thoughts, and carried them off. Splat. The droplets fell from the darkened clouds above and a drip landed on my wrist where parallel lines ran. I watched as the water worked its way into the divots of my flesh until it rolled through and then off, falling into the deep chlorophyll-green grass below. The ink from my notebook bled. I looked up and let the rain assault my cheeks until I no longer noticed its pelting.

High school dropout high school dropout high school dropout. What's wrong with me? One month left of school and I dropped out, again.

I close my eyes and
feel the blades of grass
beneath my skin,
the cool air
on the back of my neck
my soul,
floats up and out of my body.
Stop. Stop. Stop.
He doesn't.
Please, stop. I don't want this.
He keeps going.
I close my eyes.
I turn my head to the side.
I let my soul leave my body.

I came back to the moment, this present, this bench, this body, this face, these raindrops, beating down on my pinkened cheeks. My darkened thoughts plucked themselves from my brain and hovered above me.

Summer air
Warped Tour
A field and a bottle
That man
And me
Relapsing
Me?
It must be my fault
Relapsing
It wouldn't have happened
If I hadn't started drinking

Again.

The wind picked up and captured them, carrying away those thoughts, those memories, those intruders, and immediately I understood.

Perhaps the wind is the gulp of the clouds, inhaling our thoughts and pressing them deep into their darkened cumulonimbus atmosphere. Perhaps the clouds carry away our sadness, our hurt, our pain, our debilitating thoughts that cling to us for life, leaching away our vitality, collecting more and more until the weight of our plight is too much to hold on to any longer, so the clouds let go, and when the rain pours down perhaps they are releasing all the pain they have collected and sending it back down into the earth, down into the chlorophyll-imbued blades.

Drip.

Drop.

Another splat.

I let them glide down my skin

plunge into the soil.

The clouds drift on.

If I were a water droplet I would like to be born in a cumulonimbus cloud; I would grow and grow and grow until I couldn't possibly grow anymore, and then I would let go, simply release and fall to the ground. Falling. Falling. Falling.

The life of a raindrop is beautiful, immortal, because even after I splat, crack, and crash, I continue on, drip down until I seep into the ground and Mother Earth absorbs me again, forever cradled by the universal mother.

I long for that kind of love.

I closed my notebook and walked home.

I had slowly started drinking again throughout the school year after I got back from Calling Lake, surrounding myself with friends and, subsequently, alcohol and weed. Laughter with friends in basements and yards with bottles to my lips was preferable to the slow gnawing sensation that rattled in my solar plexus in those moments when I was alone.

I feared those moments, as reels from the past flickered beneath my eyelids: *blades to flesh to ease the pain.*

No. I was better than that. I would not slide back to self-harm.

A different kind of sliding took its place until it landed me in the heat of summer, sabotaging my relationship with my sisters, never wanting to be home unless I was sleeping, and behaving miserably to myself and my family.

I had slipped back into old tendencies, old patterns of using substances to lessen the pain I felt inside.

I am not worthy of love.

I am not worthy of honesty.

I am not worthy of respect.

I am not worthy of love from a trustworthy human being.

I am not worthy to stay with.

I am unlovable.

These were the fears embedded deep within my core.

I needed to confront my past. The only way I was truly going to heal myself, heal what the substances covered up, was to feel the pain, welcome it, overcome it, diminish it—I did not want to drown it but obliterate its darkness with my light. I needed to become light again, but in order to do that, I needed to confront my darkness.

Frank.

So I packed a duffle bag and bought a ticket for a Greyhound bus heading to the West Coast—the salty shores where I was born. The salty spirits that held my father.

My aunty Danielle, one of my father's younger sisters, agreed to let me live with her for a while. I was excited to see her and my little cousins I hadn't seen since I was a little girl. Would they even remember me? Was I still the girl who put on an oversized clown suit and danced and slid around the kitchen to elicit their laughter and rolling bellies on the linoleum floor?

It was an overnight bus, so I stood in the station with my mother, worry betraying her eyes, as the dark sky brought out the nocturnal beings of downtown Edmonton. Men with dirty boots and grease-stained denim shirts, the stench of stale tobacco stuck to their beards; young women with small children with tangled hair; ironworkers and people fleeing whatever they were trying to escape, all nomads.

Did I look like someone who was trying to escape?

Perhaps our only shared trait was a look in our eyes: longing tinged with a hint of loss, and the ever-so-slightest glimmer of hope.

"Are you sure you want to do this, my girl?"

"I am."

"It's not too late to turn back, you know. We can eat the cost of the ticket."

"You always knew at some point that I was going to do this. The time is now, Mom."

Her eyes welled up with fear and sadness, but also understanding.

"I'm not leaving forever, you know."

"I know... You've always marched to the beat of your own drum, and I know nothing I say now will all of a sudden change who you are, or change what you need to do and where you need to go."

"I'll be home before you know it."

"I hope so." She hugged me super tight, squeezing tears out of her eyes and mine. "Be smart, my girl. Keep your eyes and ears open and sit close behind the driver. Be sure to call me at every rest stop and let me know as soon as you get there."

"I will."

"I love you."

"I love you, too." We hugged one last time. I picked up my duffle bag and headed toward the bus that was bound for British Columbia, the nerve centre of the spirits of the salt, the place I hadn't been since I was there with him, with my mother and sisters—all of us together.

I was only seventeen, but us together as a family felt like a lifetime ago, a different world, a distant dream. For the past five years, I had only been capable of thinking of the trauma, the rupture:

the jumpsuit,

his tears,

running from the stand,

my tears,
the drugs,
the pain,
the bottles,
the boys,
and the anger.
So much anger.

For the past five years I had lived in a consistent state of being high, numbing myself, not wanting or ready to confront the one thing I knew I needed to in order to begin to move on successfully with my life.

The one person.

I stared out the dirty window of the bus. There was a chill to the air that only comes at the end of August in Alberta. It was beginning to sprinkle and I watched the rain wet the windows, creating prisms of light, bouncing off the cars and streetlights of downtown Edmonton.

The bus revved and I was jolted out of my reverie. I put in my headphones and let my iPod control my thoughts for me. I believe songs have the power to capture the essence of the unique moments of our lives; the right songs found at the right moments become pivotal accompaniments to the poignant instances that shape us. My favourite song came on: "World at Large" by Modest Mouse—a melancholic melody about drifters who feel as if there is no place they belong, leaving and searching for something, somewhere, that will make them feel full. There is a part about packing your belongings and heading to the West Coast because the thoughts inside your head have become too loud to hear anything else. It was as if this song was singing for me, to me, and encouraging me to turn toward the part in my story that I needed to outlast.

At some point I drifted to sleep, and when I woke up, I wasn't anxious. Something about this moment felt destined, predetermined, and just outright necessary. I was ready for this. I needed it. I was excited to see my aunts, uncles, grandparents, and cousins who had been stolen away from me for the past five years. I missed them.

Not only had Frank destroyed our family, but he had punished his own at the same time. How could I be in contact with his sisters, his brothers, his nieces and nephews? That proximity seemed too close, too much, too raw. But it hurt me to put them at a distance for so many years.

The bus arrived at the station and I hopped off wearing an oversized green Mexican Baja hoodie and harem pants covered in ohm symbols, with my curly dark brown hair tied up in a half-pony, and a septum ring through my nose. I peered around the lot until I saw her. My aunty Danielle, a tall, big, beautiful woman with the softest hugs but the loudest voice. I hadn't seen her in almost ten years, but in her face I saw the prominent Logan genes that are present in all of our faces. My aunty scooped me up in a big bear hug and I was stunned at how effortless it felt.

I let myself fall deeper into her hug and we both began to cry.

During my visit, I spent time with my little cousins and we went shopping in downtown Vancouver. It was nice to be with them all again and to meet the younger ones for the first time. I went out drinking with my aunty Ahchakos once, and then politely declined when they all started popping MDMA. I hiked the Grouse Grind with my uncle Justin and we took pictures together near waterfalls and let nature absorb the silences that we weren't sure how to fill. I saw my paternal grandparents for the first time since I was a little girl; Grandma Shelly made fry bread and it tasted just as good as I remembered. I sat on her sofa with my grandpa Frank across from me and made small talk.

We all avoided the topic of Frank, what he was up to, or where he was.

I knew he lived there, though—someplace in the Vancouver area.

He was the last person I wanted to see.

Needed to see.

It was a grey day, the kind where you feel the rain in the air before it falls out of the clouds.

I stared out the bay window of aunty Danielle's home and my heart thundered. I watched the sky as the clouds grew darker, and within moments I saw a black SUV pull up in the driveway.

I hadn't seen him in more than five years.

His blood and flesh permeate my body, but I had never felt more dissociated from any other person than in that moment.

It was time to put on my raincoat. I had taken special care when applying my makeup and ensured not a single hair on my head was out of place. It was silly, but I still wanted him to be proud of me. Proud of the young woman I had become, without him.

Every thought occupying my mind, each emotion, each preplanned sentence I thought I would say floated away as I drifted toward his vehicle and the first thing I saw were his eyes. They had a dark ring around the coloured irises, just like mine. Inside that dark ring was liquid amber, though his are darker than mine, darker than I remembered them to be. They were glassy as he pulled me in for an apprehensive hug, my body stiff. I awkwardly patted him on the back as all my defences brickwalled.

I wonder if he felt the bricks.

His body was thicker than I remembered, his tattoos a little faded, but his face—his face was still half of mine, and even though I didn't want to recognize anything of myself in him, there I was. There he was.

"I've missed you so much, Chy-Chy."

"I... I know. I have a lot to ask you."

I had missed him too. I hated myself for not being above that.

"I have a spot in mind where we can go. We used to go there when you were a little girl, before we moved to Alberta." He started the engine, a tear falling from his buffalo eyes.

My tears stayed locked tight inside.

"Sure, that sounds good. Where is it? I just have to text Aunty Danielle where we're going."

"Bear Creek Park."

The clouds accumulated and soon enough there was rain

on the windshield. It was hard to pay attention to what he was saying past the beating of my heart. He was talking about the area we were driving through. "That's Surrey Memorial over there, where you were born."

The rain kept falling.

"That's Burnaby out that way. We lived there for a bit when you were just a baby."

The wipers kept on.

I was talking—falling into a pattern, too scared of the silence to not say something. We parked the car and began to walk.

There is nothing quite like petrichor.

It reminds me of childhood.

It reminds me of my mother and sisters running with bare feet through a field.

It reminds me of a time when my parents were still together.

It reminds me of one of the good days.

The perfect blend of cedar and rain.

It's sweet.

We approached an old red cedar that had fallen many years ago; covered in moss, it lay perfectly horizontal, begging to be climbed upon. He hopped up first. I hopped up right after him and we both knew that this was the moment. The time for small talk was over.

Silence.

"How... how could you do it?"

He started to cry. Through muffled tears, he said, "I was... sick. I was sick and twisted and not right. I victimized your hearts, souls, bodies, and minds. I will never forgive myself for what I did to you, and Orleane, and your mother and Chayla."

I watched him cry on the red cedar in the rain and I didn't shed a single tear.

THE EIGHTH STEP is the drum closing ceremony. The Elder leads the drumming and the song. We walk up to the fire, bringing our drums with us, holding them to the crackling flames, and we release a big scream, letting it all out and letting it go and releasing it to the fire as the flames warm and tighten and prep the drum for its heartbeat. A brown woman with thick skin lets out the loudest and most painful cry I have ever heard and I cannot imagine the weight of all she must be carrying. We step back into our places in the circle and begin to beat, matching the flickering hearth and the heartbeat of the Elder's drum.

The vibration takes new shape, pulling me inside its beat.

YĀKOWAGUMEW means water with sand suspended in it—a moment in between moments, a merging of two worlds that holds a pause before settling into what is still to come.

After meeting with Frank, I felt like those grains of sand, caught within the ambivalence of one part of me that still loved my father, a small part of me wondering if there could be a world where we could exist together, and then the other part of me, the stronger part, the one I knew I would not turn away from—the love of my sister and the hurt I felt for what he did to her and to all of us. I was a seventeen-year-old girl grappling with that ambivalence, a girl who felt like a grain of sand, suspended between two worlds: the world where my father used to be a part of my life, and the world in which Frank no longer could be.

I lingered in the suspension, letting the water hold me, supporting me like my bones, until I hopped on another bus back to Alberta.

Liminal spaces are never meant to keep us for long.

It was time for me to go home, to my family—to my sister.

I AM IN A JEEP and my mother is driving and Nohkôm is sitting shotgun. Me and my two sisters are in the back. I am fourteen years old and we are driving along a gravel road, heading north on St. Albert Trail toward the acreage. The acreage where I used to build miniature teepees from sticks and climb swaying trees with thumbtacks stuck in the bark.

I stare out the window at the sky.

What is a heartbeat if not a drum.

Part III

Pâstâsow

She Breaks Bones for Marrow

WUSKOWAGUMIPUYEW is when the water moves, and as babies, all we can do is exist in the body of water where we are conceived—merely float and swim before breaking the barrier and emerging on the other side.

I met a woman on a balcony smoking a cigarette overlooking the Pacific Ocean in Shirahama, Japan. She told me that in China they have a word for the things we inherit while we are still in the womb—that protective embryonic sac of water cradling us before birth. She called it mu fu. I looked the word up later and *mu* translates to "tent" or "curtain," and *fu* denotes "home." What is a womb if not the original protective home we all have?

Research has shown that our experiences in the womb influence our attachment styles and behaviours long after we're born. I often think of myself inside my mother when my father pressed a gun to her head and she begged for our lives. The intense fear my mother must have felt in that moment—is it possible it seeped through and found its way into me? Rendering in me a predisposition to anxiety before I was even born? Perhaps those experiences in the womb led to my innate intuition for danger?

As children, we cannot control how or when the water moves—all we can do is drift and float in the tides until the day we leave them, and when that time comes, who will we be? Who will we have to reshape ourselves into?

US CREE AND MÉTIS, we call him Wîsahkêcâhk. In other Indigenous cultures he may be known as Coyote, or Raven. Wîsahkêcâhk is a trickster who can also shift shapes. No one really knows what Wîsahkêcâhk looks like, because he carries supernatural abilities that allow him to change form, reshaping himself in moments when he must become something else. He also speaks the languages of all the animals, and even plants.

He is a benevolent jokester, playing tricks on all his siblings on earth. He is mischievous, getting into all sorts of trouble, but all Wîsahkêcâhk stories have a moral, much like European fairy tales and fables—but less like Disney, and more like the Brothers Grimm, if the characters in those stories held a strong personal relationship with the land and natural world.

Wîsahkêcâhk stories are often told in the winter, as they help bring levity to the long, cold months in the prairies. Wîsahkêcâhk is not evil or bad, even though Christian morality has seen him as such. He is our trickster, and we are meant to learn from his mistakes.

He is a spirit who transforms and reshapes, learning each time.

PUPÚKIPĀSTOW is when the rain falls gently, like those quiet moments when you're sitting on a porch and the pavement is slowly bespeckled and you marvel at Mother Nature's dappled canvas—when I met the Man Who Taught Me How to Trust, it was the most gentle rain of all.

I was in grade twelve and he was the most beautiful man I had laid eyes on. I went to a house party that was a snapshot of the 1970s: an orange shag carpet beneath a haze of marijuana smoke and stale liquor. And him, sitting on a couch. He wore a ripped band tee, and his chin-length brown hair stuck out from beneath a backward snapback. I watched him tilt a can of Lucky beer to his lips. His bluebell eyes squinted through the haze in a laugh that brought a hint of a smile to my lips as I tipped my own beer can up to meet them. The coppery taste lingered on my tongue, but I detected notes of something else.

A quickening of the heart can be likened to the taste of lead piercing the tongue.

Before meeting him, I loved my patterns. Patterns are easy to follow and they leave room for no surprises. The Man Who Taught Me How to Trust threw a wrench in those patterns, a necessary breakdown to help me move beyond them. I had to shove down the moths that were fluttering around my tummy when I saw him because moths couldn't be trusted. Their movements are unpredictable, volatile. They land on you, leaving dust in their wake.

I preferred men with forgettable names and forgettable faces so that when I woke up the next day, I would be on my way and their traces were so faint they never came with me. I was seventeen when I perfected how to take what I want and leave the rest. Men were nothing more than walking, breathing trust falls guaranteed to fail, and I never gave them the power to drop me. Frank had already taught me that, hadn't he? For Frank, love was a reward, a manipulation tactic to secure my silence. I would never let another man get close.

And yet, when I met the Man Who Taught Me How to Trust, I couldn't stop myself from succumbing to his leady taste, overpowered by the dizzying pull of oxytocin and dopamine. The brain in love is very similar to the brain in the throes of addiction. Brain-imaging research has shown that when a person is feeling intense love, there is activity in the nucleus accumbens, the same area of the brain that lights up when someone is addicted to cocaine or gambling. Love can feel all-consuming because the area of the brain that produces dopamine, firing up when we are in love, is next to the area that controls thirst and hunger, meaning there is a survival element to the way our brain processes love. These drives spur us into action and into the arms of the person we love—releasing oxytocin and vasopressin, making us feel love, attachment, and a desire to protect the ones we love.

When my body was next to his, I didn't want to walk away. His blue eyes were far too happy, far too pure. But if I were a flower then I was born to the filth, soil laced with deceit, and when I stared into that man's hurricane eyes, I was scared they would storm into my carefully constructed island. His lips pressed against mine, and I felt a slight bite when his teeth grazed my lip piercings. I sighed and left the party.

We didn't speak for a year, the year when I confronted my father in Bear Creek Park. The following summer my friend Stephanie and I were in my bathroom getting ready to go out.

"What should we do tonight?" I poured us both a shot of Jim Beam while we smeared kitty-cat eyeliner above our lids. I'd started drinking again, but with a little more self-control, no blackouts.

"Should I text C and see what those guys are up to?" Steph played "House of the Rising Sun" on her iPod as she took out her red Samsung slider phone, identical to mine.

"Yeah, might as well!" I slammed back Jim and he burned his way down my throat.

"Okay, they're gonna pick us up!" Steph said, and she told me the Man Who Taught Me How to Trust would be there.

My moths fluttered. "Oh god, oh god, oh god! I haven't seen him in a year! Fuck, what should I wear?" Steph laughed as I ran frantically to the basement to find an outfit. I came running back up the stairs. "How's this?"

"You look sick, I love that shirt."

I wore a loose light grey tank top with *Slayer* written

across the front, a skin-tight black skirt, and sheer tights. I smeared on some Kat Von D liquid matte lipstick in Bambie. We took another shot and headed to the front step to have a toke before they picked us up. As I laced up my combat boots, C's white truck honked out front.

Back to the shag-carpet house we went. We spent the night drinking whisky, smoking weed, and listening to Rise Against. I sat on the Man Who Taught Me How to Trust's lap, laughing and looking into his happy red eyes, singing along to the lyrics. The night was a blur, but an underlying feeling of happiness lingered.

The next morning, I wore the Man Who Taught Me How to Trust's No Use for a Name hoodie, since he'd ripped the *Slayer* shirt off the night before.

He kissed me goodbye. "I'll text you later, okay?"

"Sounds good."

I stepped out of C's truck, moths assaulting my belly.

The next day, the Man Who Taught Me How to Trust asked me out to the movies. He was going to pick me up at 6 p.m. from work, a hybrid clothing, tattoo, and piercing shop called Divine. That morning, the sun was beaming high and the sky was a soft, gentle blue. The best hug is the one you get from the sun when it blankets you like the most familiar lover you never want to escape. I welcomed the embrace of summer, smelled the drifting lilacs, and listened to Jimi Hendrix on my iPod as I walked to work through the Edmonton River Valley, wearing a vintage black sundress with daisies all over it.

This was the day that broke my patterns, and unleashed

some more. My first date with him: the happy man with happy eyes.

Finally, the clock struck six and I said goodbye to my co-workers and went running up the stairs onto the heart of Whyte Avenue. I was greeted by warm air, wafting cigarette smoke, and bustling passersby on the cobblestone sidewalk. I saw him walking toward me and he scooped me up in his comforting six-foot-two grand hug.

"You look beautiful! Are you ready to go?"

"Ready, Freddy!" I beamed back at him.

As we approached the doors of the movie theatre, a car pulled up and the driver whistled. "Woooo, lucky guy you are!" he hollered.

"Haha, I know," said the Man Who Taught Me How to Trust.

Sometimes it's when things don't work out that they end up working out. The movie we wanted to see was sold out, so I said, "How about we just grab some food, and then we can go to my place and rent a movie on my Xbox?"

"Sure, that works! We'll just have to see this movie another time." He winked.

We pulled up to my house and sitting on the front step was my little sister, her friends, and the Neighbour Boy.

Two weeks before my date with the Man Who Taught Me How to Trust, the Neighbour Boy told me, "I want you to marry me and have my babies."

Before the Man Who Taught Me How to Trust, I had a type. Sex was a hollow comfort, and the more the other person was infatuated with me, the better it was. I was trying to fill a void inside myself, pacify the little voice that didn't believe I was worthy of love. The Neighbour Boy was one of the boys I could never love.

"But we're so young," I protested, knowing I had to cut him free. The next day, I asked him to meet me on the front step. "I'm sorry, but I can't do this anymore," I said. "I think we should stop seeing each other."

"How can you say that? Don't do this." Tears welled. "I love you, Chyana."

"I just don't love you like that. I'm so sorry."

He began to sob. "Please, I can't lose you. Please ..." He grabbed for my hand.

"You have to go." He wouldn't leave the steps, so I backed away. He was crying and begging, still grasping for me. I shook him off. "I'm sorry. We can still be friends. I still care for you." I took one last look at his leaking eyes and went inside. I listened to his sniffles through the door for a while longer.

My sisters were sitting on the couch. "Did you do it?"

"Yeah, I felt so bad. I've never seen a boy cry that much." Though a boy did once break his skateboard against a skating rink because I told him I didn't want to date him.

The next weekend, I came home hammered. I hiccupped up the steps, and there was the Neighbour Boy, smoking a joint on his front step.

"Hey, what's u-up?" I slurred.

"Holy, someone had fun tonight, haha." He inhaled deeper.

I invited him inside. He crawled in through my window and I used his body to fill the void. It was wrong, and I knew it, but I did it anyway. After, I told him, "You should go."

The next time I saw him, I was pulling up in the passenger seat of the Man Who Taught Me How to Trust's car. When I saw the Neighbour Boy sitting on the front step with my little sister and some of her friends, I panicked, not wanting him to see me with a new guy so soon. I suggested we drive around to the back, even though never in my life had we ever parked in the alley. By the time we got there, everyone had migrated to the backyard, and I had to parade my new guy in front of the old one, up the back steps, and down into my room.

As soon as we got into my basement, though, all the awkwardness faded away as he marvelled at my walls that were splattered with painted lines of my poetry, paintings, and drawings. Coming into my space meant glimpsing my soul in fragments, and even though I'd had many parties with friends in this basement, this was the first time I'd welcomed a boy into it dead sober, on something as formal as a first date.

The Man Who Taught Me How to Trust moved through my space, taking in each poem, each picture, each memory. I felt like he was seeing all sides of me, quickly, quicker than I would usually reveal, and for a moment I felt exposed, but when I saw the kindness in his eyes, filled with awe and wonder, my guard lowered, and before long, I was guiding him through the room, answering all his questions, revealing more and more about the meaning of the words and images on my walls. It was easy to be open with him. I didn't tell him everything, but I told him a lot.

We eventually watched a movie and he didn't try to make a single move on me. That was a first. After the movie, we cuddled, laughed, and talked, until we realized it was four in the morning. I walked him to my front steps and he sat there with me as I smoked a cigarette, cherry glowing in the pitch of night. We hugged and he gave me the most perfect kiss. I hadn't kissed a boy sober or not hungover in more than a year.

I watched him walk to his car, and in that moment, I knew I loved him already.

After six months of dating I finally said those words to him. My heart was in my stomach, as I waited to hear if he would say them back. He did. I got to know his parents and adored them. His father shared the same birthday as Frank, and for the first time in a long time this day became something worth celebrating. Through the Man Who Taught Me How to Trust's family, I healed parts of myself and gained things I had lacked as a child. A couple more months went by and he asked me to move in with him and his family. I jumped in with both feet, ready to be immersed in his world.

His world had been perfectly formed from the moment he was born, and mine had been a tangled web of destruction from the moment Frank pointed a gun at my mother's head. The Man Who Taught Me How to Trust was everything that I wasn't. He was electric down to his bass guitar and long salt-and-pepper hair that peeked out from behind his backward hat—I was thunder that was undetectable until I was in his presence.

Love was hard for me, or rather, trust was hard for me,

and how can you possibly love without trust? Trust was easy for him. The Man Who Taught Me How to Trust loved without question, without condition, without expectation. I loved from darkness, a void wanting to be filled, hungry. He tried so hard to shine his light on me. I needed my first true love to be someone like him, with a heart so untainted, so trustworthy, so giving, and so humble. Effortlessly honest. Effortlessly good. Not perfect, but perfect for loving me the way he did. He never made me feel less than, even if at times I was. I had never opened up to anyone before, always protecting myself, keeping others at a distance, deciding anyone trying to enter my life was a threatening invader. I defended myself within the walls I had built around me, walls that kept me isolated.

He showed me that it could be safe to open my heart to another.

Even still, because he was the first man I let into my heart, I could never give him all of it—as much as I wanted to. We can only meet people as far as we have met ourselves, and at that time, I was the most healed I had ever been, but still miles and years from where I am today.

We can only heal so much of ourselves on our own, learning to be comfortable in our aloneness until it is time to welcome another into the beautiful lives we have cultivated for ourselves, sharing and growing together, influencing and inspiring each other, supporting one another in all the ways we previously wouldn't have known how to.

When I met the Man Who Taught Me How to Trust, I had not yet learned how to be comfortable in that aloneness, but I can see now how that had to come later, because during this period of my life, the lesson I needed to learn was how to be close to another person without sabotaging the bond, without being the reaper of my own self-fulfilling prophecy.

He gave me hope that not all men have ulterior motives; not all men would put me in the palm of their hand and suffocate me until my innards popped and splattered everywhere. It was an honour to be loved by him. He healed so much within me until I could heal outward, growing wiser and further, until the only thing left to do was break free of him.

EHKASKAWANPESTAK is when it is drizzling rain, and it is only a matter of time before standing in the middle of the drizzle will eventually take its toll, each drop falling heavier and heavier until the weight of the ocean pours down.

After two years together, I had fallen back into old patterns of drug use.

It started one night when the Man Who Taught Me How to Trust tried cocaine for the first time. I didn't want to be left out. *What the hell, I'll do it with him this once,* I thought. That was the new danger I was learning from loving the Man Who Taught Me How to Trust—I wanted to do everything with him, be with him all the time, even when his activities became detrimental to what I needed. He was a life raft that I happily jumped onto after leaving my own family, moving in with his, and making his life mine.

Hadn't I wanted this? Hadn't I wanted to run away from my own life and into a brand-new one?

But my entire relationship was structured around partying. I worked at the Liquor Depot, and then each weekend invested my money back into the place I earned it from. I knew it was time to start thinking about my future career.

Throughout my life, I had always been writing. As soon as I learned how, I was writing songs, which evolved into poetry, which evolved into fiction, all of which encompassed my non-fiction. I wanted to pursue my dream of becoming a writer and a creative writing professor. I started researching programs and set my sights on the University of Alberta. Once I turned twenty-one, I could apply as a mature student, meaning I wouldn't need a high school diploma. Meanwhile, I took classes to upgrade my coursework during the day, worked at the Liquor Depot at night, and then drank all weekend at C's with the Man Who Taught Me How to Trust.

This is what I had been doing for the last four years, and only in the last year had drinking escalated to drugs. At first, I was using drugs just one weekend here or there, but then, before I knew it, every weekend at C's house turned into a big drug fest. Cocaine, MDMA, mushrooms, acid, ketamine, you name it. I knew deep down that I couldn't sustain this any longer, but these people were my friends, and they were the only ones I had, through no one's choice but my own. They were the best friends of the man I loved, the man I stayed up late with, laughing, playing video games, sneaking snacks in the wee hours of the morning, sitting in cars, and speaking our own language that only we could understand. What would I do each weekend if not hang out with them?

It all culminated on the night I hit the floor.

I spent the whole night in C's basement and we were all on MDMA. I sat on a couch for four straight hours smoking joint after joint and drinking glass after glass of water, all while not using the bathroom and barely moving around.

"We should probably try to go to bed. The sun is coming up and I'm starting to feel the comedown," I finally told the Man Who Taught Me How to Trust.

"Yeah, I'm starting to come down too. Let's go sleep upstairs in C's room."

I got up from the couch and floated up the stairs, but when I reached the top my vision started to blur and before I could understand what was happening, I fell to the ground. The Man Who Taught Me How to Trust was right behind me and was able to catch me and guide me to the floor. I was awake, breathing, but my vision was gone, blinded. Like when a TV goes to static.

I was twenty years old when I collapsed on the floor and couldn't get up. Every time I looked at the Man Who Taught Me How to Trust, parts of his face were lost in the static and I was convinced that I would never be the same again. He tried to help me off the floor, but I couldn't move. I was immobilized, and not from fear—my brain was not sending the correct messages and my body was not responding. C and some of our friends tried to help me up, but nothing was working. I was not working.

About forty minutes later they were about to call an ambulance. In hindsight, it should have been called the moment I hit the ground, but a house full of drugs makes people a little reluctant. Finally, I was able to push myself up onto my forearms and crawl to the bathroom a few feet away, while the Man Who Taught Me How to Trust guided me.

As soon as I got to the toilet I started throwing up buckets and buckets of water. Every time I threw up, parts of my vision came back. All night I had been drowning myself from the inside without realizing it. After thirty minutes, I regained consciousness, vision, and bodily coordination.

I went to bed and when I woke up I did an internal scan of my body and was thankful when I was able to wiggle my legs and arms, and then push myself out of bed. I prayed, for the first time in a long time, thanking Creator and the universe.

I never wanted to experience that again.

After that night, I started having panic attacks and developed an anxiety disorder. I could no longer lie to myself. I realized how precious my life was, my physical health, the ability to see, to move my body—to feel, feel, feel. I didn't just *want* to change my life again, I *needed* to. Time was up.

For most of my relationship with the Man Who Taught Me How to Trust, I had stopped writing. I had been so focused on my relationship and improving myself within it that I had been neglecting my own personal development. It was time that stopped. I needed to start growing on my own.

I had made his life my life.

I didn't want it anymore.

The next few months moved fast and slow, melding together in a dance between the crippling pull of anxiety and my desire to defeat it. I was enrolled in the last course I needed before I could apply to university. I got a new job in the customer service department at the Running Room, but I would often have to come home early because the room would start spinning and my heart racing. I would be disoriented, dizzy, and have to sit on the ground and breathe to try to convince myself that I wasn't about to die. So much of this period I spent sitting on the bathroom floor, hovering above the toilet, dry heaving and sweating while my heart raced and the room swirled. The Man Who Taught Me How to Trust tried to help me, but he didn't know what to do.

One day I was throwing up in the toilet while he rubbed my back, trying to reassure me that I wasn't dying.

"I need my mom," I said. "I need you to call her right now."

My mom made me feel safe. Always has.

Once I called her when I was having a bad mushroom trip and she came and picked me up. The second I got into her car, I felt okay. All my fear and anxiety melted away.

She drove to the townhouse I was living in with the Man Who Taught Me How to Trust and two of his friends. She rubbed my back, drew me a bath, and helped me calm down. She smudged the townhouse and then me with sage and sweetgrass. She set me up on the couch with a hot water bottle and a blanket, and made me peppermint tea and hot toddies, sans whisky.

Who had I become? Who was the girl with scared eyes and a racing heart and blurry vision ... I was not the person I knew myself to be. I was not writing.

I realized how far away from myself I had gotten. After that I started smudging and journalling every day, things I had stopped doing for the past few years. I made a commitment to find myself again and only do what was good for my body. I started a yoga challenge and for thirty straight days I showed up to that mat, even when my heart was racing. I pushed through the crippling anxiety and reconnected my mind with my body and stopped running away from the uncomfortable feelings inside. I sat with them, acknowledged them, and pushed through my fear of them. I aligned my breath with my mind, my spirit, my movement—an embodiment of all four houses of the medicine wheel in one practice.

After a month, my panic attacks started to lessen, from every day, to every other day, to a couple times a week. I realized I would have a panic attack if I was hungover, so I stopped drinking for a whole year, slowly introducing social drinking after I felt better, more healed. If I smoked weed? Anxiety. So I stopped that too. I had been smoking weed every day of my life since I was eleven years old, with the exception of stints of sobriety that lasted no longer than a couple of weeks. For the first time in my life, weed created my anxiety instead of calming it. I could no longer handle any altered state of mind without being brought back to that night when I hit the floor. That night, I had felt a complete and total lack of control over my body, and it was a feeling I never wanted to experience again.

After I finally got a handle on my panic attacks and was feeling more in control of my body again, I was sitting at my desk at work one day when I got an email about my application to the University of Alberta. My heart skipped a beat as I raced to open it. My eyes scanned the screen until I saw the word that would begin to shape the rest of my life: *accepted*. I was twenty-one years old.

I leapt from my chair and started jumping for joy. My co-worker joined in and I started crying. I called my mom immediately to tell her the news and we cried together over the phone. After years of neglecting myself and the thing that made me the most happy—writing—I was finally ready to start chasing my dreams and begin my bachelor's degree studying English and creative writing.

MANY MOONS AGO, deep in the boreal forest, Wîsahkêcâhk was taking a walk. He loved to smell the sap from the birches and would march up to the bark, placing his nose right against a tree so he could take a deeper breath.

A bluebird saw what he was doing and told him, "Wîsahkêcâhk, you should be careful not to get too close to the sap. It's quite sticky and you might get some in your eyes!"

"Nonsense, Bluebird! The sap is good for my skin, you know."

The bluebird just chirped away in response, disregarding Wîsahkêcâhk's carelessness once again. As Wîsahkêcâhk walked through the forest, he kept smelling the trees, sap building up on his face and near his eyes. The sky was growing darker and darker until he could barely see a thing. He waved his hands in front of his face, but he couldn't make out a single finger.

"My hands, my hands!" he cried out. "Where have they gone?"

He heard a rustling close by and decided to walk toward the noise, determined to find someone who could help him. He finally found where the noise was coming from, but all he could see was two eyes lit up in the dark. Wîsahkêcâhk walked toward them until he felt an animal's soft fur in front of him and, in the moonlight, could see it shining. He was relieved to still be able to feel something. He had felt an animal like this before, and he knew it was his friend—the black Labrador who often ran through the woods, jubilant and blissful.

"Oh, Labrador! I am so happy to have found you..."

"Wîsahkêcâhk, why do you look so frightened?"

"I think I must have lost my hands while I was walking through the forest. Have you seen them anywhere?"

"I don't think I've seen them anywhere, Wîsahkêcâhk, but I just felt them when you touched me. I think you still have them."

"But I can't see my hands, so surely they must have fallen off!"

Labrador looked at Wîsahkêcâhk, but where he should

have seen eyes, he just saw brown goop. "Wîsahkêcâhk, I think you must have lost your eyes, because I cannot see them. It looks like they fell out."

"My eyes?! Oh dear, it's even worse than I thought," Wîsahkêcâhk said.

"I might have something that could help you."

Wîsahkêcâhk felt relieved, because all he wanted was to see clearly again.

"I have these two magical seeds, and if you plant them in your sockets, then you will grow new eyes and be able to see everything in the world and more."

Wîsahkêcâhk was over the moon. "Oh, my friend! Please place them in my hands and I will plant them at once!"

The black Labrador placed the two seeds in Wîsahkêcâhk's palms and watched as he placed one in each socket. It kind of stung a little bit, like when a piece of dust gets in your eyes. Immediately, Wîsahkêcâhk felt the seeds take root, and he waited, eager for what his new eyes would be able to see.

KIMIWANISIW means it has rain, it receives rain, and she is caught in the rain, but there are many different ways to be under the rain, caught in it, submerged—there are moments when all you want is the rain to beat down upon your skull and carry all your worries into the soil with it, and then there are moments when the rain is strong, too strong, and you don't really want it, but there it is, and you can't get away from it.

Silly human, don't you know that people can't be lifeboats? One time, I made a mistake, turning his flesh, his bones, his mind into my home.

When the day came to turn around and walk away, I realized I was leaving behind my home. my solace. my comfort.

But he was not mine to make, so I staggered away, stealing one last g l a n c e at the man who picked up my broken pieces, put me together, and sent me back out into the world, where I belonged.

At twenty-two years old, my first year of university done, I broke up with the Man Who Taught Me How to Trust. One night, I walked into a bathroom stall at Avenue nightclub and shut the sticky metal door behind me. Orleane followed me in and took a small vial out of her bra. She tapped white powder onto the back of my hand where the thumb meets the index finger. I plugged one nostril as I inhaled deeply through the other. She took one for herself, and then I had another. We walked out of the stall and over to the mirror. I looked into my large brown eyes as I smeared some lip gloss on my lips.

I paused at the hypocrite in the mirror staring back at me with amber eyes.

I did not fall in love with that man; rather, it was a slow and steady stroll. Letting him go was much the same. It didn't happen overnight and there wasn't a specific moment where I felt our relationship end, not truly. Each step I took in the direction of not drinking, not doing drugs, going to school, making new friends, inviting him along—*join me*, and his answer always, *I'm going to C's*—all led me further and further away until eventually the inner cord that connected me to him was stressed and taut.

I looked back at him and knew
the only way for me to go forward
was to cut the cord,
but knowing that it had to be done
did not render my love obsolete;
knowing it had to be done
didn't kill me any less.

The night I told him I didn't love him anymore, I watched the light that helped give me mine dissolve behind closed midnight doors. Once upon a time, I made him my lifeboat. Now he was trying to make me his. But the person that had been with him died when she found herself.

I told him, people can't be lifeboats.

I shut my apartment door, locked it, slid down the frame, resting at the bottom, tears salting my shoulders and splashing my collarbone. His face embedded behind my eyelids, when I watched his light flicker out.

"I don't love you anymore." I needed him to believe it.

But there was still one more time—isn't there always when you say goodbye to the person you loved for four years?

I knocked on the Man Who Taught Me to Trust's door, and he opened it. We walked into another room, one that this world couldn't see or touch. We sat at a small table across from one another, staring past a flickering candle flame and into eyes we knew so well. Sipping my wine, and drinking his beer, our voices emerged, but our eyes communicated—a familiar memorized dance.

He talked about her, and I talked about him, but we could feel that impending pull, silently hoping that the present would one day be the past and the future would be ours again. He held my hand over the table and my eyes betrayed my lips, and with a quiver and a whimper I started to break the rule—

"Do you think one day you could love me again?"

"Don't ask me that question when you made me close the door."

His eyes asked how that could be possible when the love never left. I smiled, apologized, and gave way to one of my giggles.

We were supposed to get up and say our goodbyes, only when we walked back to the door leading to the hallway that separated our lives—we did the unimaginable. I should've licked my wounds and collapsed on my side of the door, but I grabbed his hand and walked into his. It was different there, but it still felt like home. He still felt like home. We played our favourite songs while I sat on his lap, steps away from what used to be our bed.

This world was ours.

We danced and played all night until the sun peeked through the curtains, reminding me that this was no longer my home.

He stared at my naked body, memorizing every detail,

because he knew that he would never look upon me again. I ran my hands along his chest, carving into memory every time I had lain upon it. Putting on my jeans, I kissed him a final time, with a final tear, and left. With a hand hovering over the handle to my door, my eyes glanced back and my hand followed.

I shook my head, turned my doorknob, and walked back into my world, without him.

But now here I was, twenty-two and fresh out of my first great love that had consumed all of me for the past four years, staring into my glazed eyes in a mirror with thumping music beating through the walls. I left my best friend, my blue-eyed hurricane boy, for the same reasons I was relapsing right now.

I am empty without him,
void of his love,
his affections;
I gobbled up
and satiated an emptiness
that I filled
in all the wrong ways.

When you leave someone you love not because you don't love them anymore but because you know they are no longer healthy for you, it is the worst kind of heartbreak.

I opened the bathroom door, allowed the music to burst forth, and marched back out into the bright lights and pounding rap music. The bartender waved us over and we washed back the medicinal taste with tequila.

I will be better tomorrow.

AS WÎSAHKÊCÂHK WAITED for his new eyes, he kept walking through the woods. With his new eyes still growing, his other senses were heightened. He could smell the trees and feel the wind more intensely. After a few days, Wîsahkêcâhk began to see clearly again. Everything had a rosy tint, like the sun was constantly setting. Labrador was right: the world was even more beautiful than before.

As he walked, Wîsahkêcâhk noticed all the animals and birds laughing at him and he couldn't understand why. He grew frustrated and started running, running, running, not wanting to be laughed at anymore.

Wîsahkêcâhk ran until he sat underneath a tree and was crying, crying, crying. The tears seemed to make his eyes hurt, deep within their sockets. Fox came by and saw Wîsahkêcâhk crying under that tree. He stopped in his tracks because he saw that instead of eyes, Wîsahkêcâhk was growing roses in their place.

Fox asked Wîsahkêcâhk, "My brother, why do you weep?"

"Everyone has been laughing at me, and all I want to do is see and smell all the nature, but for some reason my eyes keep hurting."

"Wîsahkêcâhk, you don't have normal eyes right now. You have roses growing inside your eye sockets."

"What?! You mean to tell me that Labrador gave me the wrong seeds?!"

"Well, that depends. Have you been able to see?"

"Why, yes ... and everything I look upon is more beautiful and wonderful than I remember it to be."

Fox knew that the rose eyes had a secret power that would prevent him from doing what Fox does best: playing tricks on his friend Wîsahkêcâhk. The roses allowed only beauty and goodness to be seen.

"If you want, I can take the roses out of your eyes, and I can help your own eyes grow back."

"Oh, Fox, you can really do that for me? Yes, please, take them out!" Wîsahkêcâhk cried.

And so Fox steadied himself against Wîsahkêcâhk and used all his might to pull out the roses. He pulled, and pulled, and pulled, until the roots and all came shooting out of the sockets! Instantly, the pain left Wîsahkêcâhk's eyes, but his vision was blurred again.

Fox could see that Wîsahkêcâhk's eyes were crusted over with birch sap, but he decided not to tell Wîsahkêcâhk and play a trick on him. After all, Wîsahkêcâhk had been playing tricks on Fox since the beginning of time.

"In order to make your eyes grow back you will have to transform into a fox."

"Oh, yes, that's a great idea! Fox, please give me your permission to turn into a fox for a while!"

And so Fox did a dance around Wîsahkêcâhk, and within moments Wîsahkêcâhk was able to transform into a fox, including his eyes. He blinked a few times and could see everything again! He ran swiftly through the woods, running back toward all the other animals who had laughed at him, and he snorted in their direction, pouncing on them as they walked by.

All the animals wondered why Fox was attacking them, but then Wîsahkêcâhk transformed back into his own body, shocking the animals into their homes. The only problem was that when Wîsahkêcâhk transformed back into himself, he kept the eyes of the fox, stuck to the sap within his sockets, so he saw the world in a sly, slick way. Whereas the roses allowed him to see all the world's beauty, the fox eyes saw only games and tricks. Fox watched on, laughing and overjoyed to have another jokester on his team.

KIMOWANAHASÎS is when a bird announces the rain, and it would be so simple, so helpful if there were a little bird that would emerge the moment before meeting someone who is not good for you—I would call it a redwing because it would sing in the presence of red flags.

I met the Charismatic Sociopath on my very first Tinder date. The first night we met we drank tea and he told me one of his friends died and I told him about my father. He sang me country love songs and wrote me poetry and from that first kiss we shared on my couch with tea in hand we spent fifty-five straight days together. He created a fairy tale around us and I wanted to jump into the pages. He took me to Lake Louise and we sat by a window in the Fairmont Chateau and watched the fluffy snowfall over the lake while drinking hot chocolate. He once filled my entire apartment with our favourite flowers and wrote love notes on all the mirrors. It was easier to be cold, but I always had a loving heart. I thought he could be the one I would stay with. I was twenty-three, with two years left of my undergrad, and he told me he wanted me to be his wife and travel the world together and I believed him.

From him I learned never to trust someone who always says the right thing. I prefer hard truths and raw revelations of the self, but back then, I let him pour his honey down my throat.

I let him talk me out of the time when a text banner from a girl with the word cum in it popped down while we were watching a video on his phone. I wanted to believe him when he said it was from a co-worker in the oil field making inappropriate jokes. Was this a red flag or my trust issues? He consistently made me believe it was my trust issues.

I wanted to believe him when he went home for the holidays and he said he couldn't talk on the phone because he was spending time with his son. I wanted to think that he placed his cellphone screen-side down on every dinner table because he didn't want to be rude or interrupt our time together.

He went home to Saskatchewan after his job ended and something started to feel wrong. His communication was too brief and too different from what was typical of him.

I hovered over the private Instagram profile of a woman named Brittney. She was the mother of his son, and from the thumbnail picture, I could make out that she was my opposite—blonde, white, blue-eyed, with an innocuous expression. She looked as if she didn't occupy too much space.

I thought back to the time I was playing *World of Warcraft* on his computer when he was away at work and a message popped down from Brittney saying that she loved him. I should have left then, but I let him sob in the hallway as I was about to leave and convince me that he didn't know why she said that to him. But finally, there were too many inconsistencies, and his words were no longer enough. I made a fake profile for a woman Brittney knew, used her Facebook profile picture, and then hit the follow button on Brittney. She accepted the request within a few hours, and in a matter of moments, the curtain was lifted. In one winded breath, the truth was on display for me to see.

There were photos of Brittney and the Charismatic Sociopath as a family, as a couple, a happy birthday post and an anniversary post. They were cute. She was cute. I realized immediately that I was the intruder, an unknowing paramour. My heart drifted up and out of my body and went someplace else.

It took me a long time to find it again.

After eight months of dating, I stopped wanting to believe and wrote myself out of his fairy tale. I had given this man almost a year of my life, and after extensive research of Brittney's profile learned that I occupied one of the four years she had spent with him.

I sent her a message: *Hi Brittney. I wanted to introduce myself...* and told her the whole story.

She replied, *Wow. Thank you for this. You literally just*

set me free. I knew he lied about you. He told me you were the girlfriend of one of his friends from work.

I texted him a screenshot of my messages with Brittney. Minutes later, he showed up at my apartment, letting himself in with the keys I had given him, which was odd because in the morning he'd told me he wouldn't be in Edmonton for a few more days.

"Please, Chyana, just listen to me," he pleaded. "I was mad at Brittney when you and I met. I only meant to get even with her. I didn't expect to fall in love with you, and then it all just got out of control."

"Get the fuck away from me," I spat. "I mean it."

Meanwhile, Brittney was sending me screenshots of some of her messages with him. I learned that he'd bought us identical Christmas presents that included earrings, Lululemon leggings, and vibrators.

"Matching vibrators!" I yelled. "Are you kidding me? What kind of sick fuck are you?"

He was inches from my face, trying to grab onto me. I brought the back of my hand down hard on the side of his cheek. For a moment, it looked like he was fighting the urge to hit me back. His face was red and swollen. "Chyana, please, stop talking to her. Stop reading those messages. I love you. I was a coward and didn't know how to end things with her. Please." He was crying.

"You need to get the fuck out of my house right now because, I swear to god, I will fucking murder you." I shoved him toward my front door. He collapsed in front of it and started sobbing into my shoes.

"Get up. You look pathetic."

"I am pathetic! Please, can't I just stay one more night? Can we have one last night together?"

"You need to leave. I can't do this." I forced my tears back inside. He looked up at me, reluctantly brought himself to his feet, and walked out my door. I locked it, slid down the frame, and started sobbing silently as I heard his truck drive away.

Brittney and I both left him. I cut up the painting he bought me that hung above my bed. I gathered the dried flowers, crumpled love notes, jewellery, clothing, and the vibrator. I shoved it all into a box and threw it in a dumpster. I sent him a picture of everything he ever gave me in the trash, and then blocked him.

Brittney and I messaged for days and uncovered every lie he ever told us. He told her he couldn't afford to fly her and his son out to visit him while he was working, and then flew me out instead. He sent us almost identical proclamations of love on our birthdays. It was hard to hear for both of us.

We leaned on each other in those early days. I wiped my hands as quickly as I could and moved on, but she shared a child with him. I felt for her. He would always be in her life in some way.

I reached out to her when I saw him three years later in Edmonton when I was at a restaurant with a couple of my girlfriends. I was sitting on the patio, wearing a peach satin romper that tied around the waist with a cute bow. The Charismatic Sociopath walked by and we made eye contact. We stared at each other, but his step did not falter and my conversation did not pause. I picked up my phone and opened Instagram.

Holy shit, Brittney, I just saw him. He isn't looking the healthiest.

Hahaha yeah, his new girlfriend is giving birth in the Royal Alexandra Hospital right now.

Poor girl. I wonder if she knows what a nightmare he is. I took a sip of my bellini and thanked the gods that wasn't me. *Who knows, maybe he's changed?* I tried to give him the benefit of the doubt.

Yeah, right. I doubt it.

Well, I hope you're well.

You too. Xox.

After the Charismatic Sociopath, I believed all men were trash, and maybe because I believed it so vehemently, I kept attracting men just like him.

NOHTEKIMIWAN is when it looks like it is going to rain, or it wants to rain—but what happens when you want to get closer to those cumulonimbus clouds that look like the most dazzling display so that you can experience the night show of lightning and the symphony of thunder?

I believe our spirit leaves us clues before we enter this world. If I lift up my left eyelid and look down, the veins on my eyeball make out a perfect letter *M*. I found it when I was fourteen and it's probably been there since the day I was born. I have always believed this letter *M* on my eyeball was one of these clues, an indicator of an essential lesson I needed to learn on my journey.

When I was twenty-four years old, in the third year of my undergraduate degree at the University of Alberta, I got a job at a gym, and that's where I met M.

I had just signed a lease on a downtown one-bedroom apartment and the gym was within walking distance. I fell in love with working out when I quit doing drugs. For me, there is and has never been any leeway. I moved out of home when I was eighteen years old and have been paying my own phone bill since I was fifteen. I have always made rent, bought my own groceries, and paid all my own bills. I have never struggled to find employment and I love working and being busy. Working out helped with my depression and anxiety, school was the goal to bettering myself and my future, and work paid the bills.

New apartment, new job, working toward a new me.

On my first day, he walked up to the front desk. "Hey, I'm M." He was a fitness consultant and had his own office toward the back of the gym.

I swivelled on my chair to face him. "Hi, I'm Chyana." I shook his outstretched hand. He had dark, long, curly eyelashes that framed his perfectly almond-shaped eyes, and short, dark brown hair with matching facial hair. He wore black pants, a black belt, and we both wore matching red collared work shirts.

"How's your first day going?" he asked.

"It's going good! Slowly getting the gist of things."

"That's good! Well, if you need anything or have any questions, I'll be around." He flashed a smile that revealed prominent canines and swooped his six-foot-two, broad-shouldered frame back to his office as quickly as he'd come.

That first Saturday, my co-workers invited me out to the bar. I got ready at my place, deciding on green camo joggers, a black bandeau top, a cropped grey sweatshirt, and brand-new white Puma sneakers. I arrived at the gym after closing to pregame and called the manager, Garett, to let me in.

"Hey Chyana! Glad you could make it," he greeted me warmly. "We're all in the back."

"Of course! Gotta get to know everyone better, you know." I smiled a little nervously and followed him toward the empty yoga studio where everyone was standing around, drinking beers and coolers and passing around a bottle of vodka. I was disappointed that M wasn't there. This other guy, B, who was a personal trainer, came up to me right away. B had long hair in a man bun, huge muscles, and a kind demeanour. Attraction lives in eye contact, and the energy that transfers between two sets determines brimstone, butterflies, swing sets, or forgotten stems in the gutter. For many people B was a catch, but for me, he was a swing set.

"Hey, I love the pants!" he said. "So, tell me, what's your story?" He clinked his beer with mine.

"Erdinger is so good!" I said, nodding to his beer. "One of my fave German beers. Ich kann ein bisschen Deutsch."

"Ah, Ich Auch! Wenn hast du gelernt?"

As I took a sip, M walked in. I glanced at him and we made eye contact. Brimstone. He was wearing a forest-green tee and black denim. His eyes could look as ferocious as a wolf's or as cuddly as a koala's, black as tourmaline or yellow as amber. His skin was olive, just like mine.

I looked back at B, hoping I hadn't looked too long at M. "Um, I'm actually studying German right now in university. I had to take a second language. French was full, and I'm part German, so I thought, what the fuck? I'll learn. Then I just fell in love with it und jetzt kann ich Deutsch." I raised my shoulders and tilted my head to the side.

I didn't hear much else that B said after that. I felt the presence of M a couple feet away. M and I ended up sitting next to each other in the Uber to Mercer Tavern, where we danced together before perching at the bar, talking and drinking.

"You sure you're not into him?" He nodded over to B.

"Hahaha, why would you think that?" I took a sip of my rye and water with a twist of lime.

"'Cause you were both speaking German. I definitely can't speak German."

"Oh, you heard that, did you?" I smiled cheekily. "I thought you barely noticed me."

"Well, I mean you were a little preoccupied with B, no?" He matched my cheekiness.

We squared our shoulders and stared deep into each other's eyes. "I'm right where I want to be." I peered up at him while taking a sip.

"I was just thinking, who the fuck is this girl? Speaking German, being so beautiful..." The wolf appeared in his eyes. "You're pretty amazing, Chy. Can I call you that? Has anyone used that nickname for you before?"

"No, they haven't. My fam calls me Chy-Chy. But you can call me Chy. I like it." I took another sip.

"You want to get out of here?"

"Yes, we can go to my place. I don't live far."

He grabbed me by the hand and led me toward the exit. B saluted me with his beer. I saluted him back.

As soon as we got in the door to my apartment, we started kissing and yanked each other's shirts off before leaving a trail of clothes to the bedroom.

The following Tuesday, he texted me: *What're you up to right now?*

I'm just watching Tokyo Ghoul. *Do you watch anime?*

Tokyo Ghoul, *huh? Is it any good? Never seen it.*

Damn, for real? It's fire. Ghouls and eating humans and shit. I think you'd vibe it.

You think so? Should I come over and watch it with you? ;)

Mmmm, still thinking of the other night, are you? ;)

Maaaaybe.

Haha, sure. Come over!

An hour later, he was at my door. He sat down on my bed and said he had something to tell me before we hooked up again.

"I want you to know that I'm seeing someone else. It's not exclusive or anything. She used to be my old roommate, but she has a boyfriend. I'm not really sure what's happening with that situation right now or what will come of it, but I wanted you to know before we do anything else. You know, if this is going to be a thing." He gestured to the space between us with a smile.

It didn't even surprise me anymore how easily people lied and cheated on their partners. I wondered how this girl would feel if she knew that I knew her dirty little secret. "Well, I appreciate you telling me. To be honest, I'm not looking for anything serious right now. I'm kind of on a mission to be single, but I would like someone to hook up with regularly. You know, a girl has needs." We both chuckled.

I had been single for the past six months, casually dating and dodging men at the first glimpse of a red flag. After my relationship with the Charismatic Sociopath, I had learned to sleuth and detect. I wanted to feel at peace with myself before inviting love into my life again. I wanted to be in a position to trust again before opening that door, but it still felt nice to be desired, and M seemed equally as detached. The way that M was honest made me think he was someone I could trust; maybe he was worth the risk.

"So, that's okay with you?" he confirmed.

"It's more than fine with me. I appreciate the honesty."

He leaned in for a kiss, and afterward we lay naked in my bed, falling asleep to anime ghouls ripping human flesh.

It was easy to be with M. We worked out together, went to the movies, and he walked me home after our late shifts, always insisting on walking on the side closest to the road. It was convenient and fun. It was also a recipe for catching feelings.

After a heavy leg day at the end of September, we were sitting across from each other at Fatburger. While he ate his cheddar and bacon and I had the mushroom Swiss, he said,

"Chy, I think Annie is going to break up with her boyfriend. We're going to actually give it a shot together." He peered deeply into my eyes while my heart sank.

Steady breaths, chew your burger. "Well, I hope it works out for you, M. I'll be happy if you're happy."

Not much changed after that conversation. We continued everything we were doing, minus the sex. We went to Denny's and ate pancakes, watched *Spider-Man: Into the Spider-Verse* when it came out, and binged sushi after hard workouts. He told me about his dad, and I told him about mine. Our fathers had the same name, but they fucked us up in different ways. We both revealed a hatred for them, fearing the things we'd inherited, and that made us feel closer to each other.

"My dad used to be pretty bad, but he always said that my mom saved his life," he told me one night. "Sometimes I don't respect my mom because of everything she does for him." M feared becoming his dad; bipolar disorder can be hereditary.

I had longed for the love of my father my whole childhood, unaware of what it meant when he gave Orleane more attention, just knowing that I was never chosen. Never quite feeling his love, but never failing to want it. I lived in my father's moving shadow, never quite grasping the person who created it. I lived for the moments Frank told me his secrets because it made me feel like I was closer to understanding everything that was being hidden from me. I enjoyed hearing M's secrets for the same reason: because it made me feel special to be privy to them, made me feel that I was special to him.

By the end of October, we had become best friends. We rarely drank alcohol together after that first night, and it was just us, conversations, food, and films. It was him who talked with me late into the night when I was crying after Orleane hurled another round of hurtful insults at me. It was him who told me that people can be like leeches and I can't let them hold me back or get me down. It was him who spent his last twenty dollars to buy us both donairs after I had a terrible night with my sister. It was nice to have him as my friend, to have a man I could depend on in a non-romantic way. Now I can see how that was still part of my problem, the way I relied on him for my happiness. He helped with my depression and I helped with his, but someone else should never be the cure for your mental health problems. The truth is that during this time of my life, when I was moving away from drinking and drug use, I didn't have many people around me other than M. The hardest part of making healthier choices is having to completely change your social circle.

In late October I went out to Central Social Hall for an old friend's birthday. At the end of the night, I took her friend back to my apartment and we made out a little. When he was in the bathroom, I texted M: *I brought a boy home. Wish me luck, friend!* He never responded.

The next day at the gym M came up to me while I was doing squats and said, "You hungover today or what?"

"Not too bad. Gotta sweat it out and I'll be chill."

On my way out after my workout, I stopped by the front desk where M was covering a co-worker's dinner break.

"So, you have fun last night?" he asked me.

"Yeah, I did, actually. It was nice to get out for the first time in a while."

"Never fucking text me something like that again." He stared at me with tourmaline eyes. "Would you like it if I texted you while Annie was over?"

From my internet stalking, I'd gathered that she hadn't broken up with her boyfriend. *It's easy to lie and hard to leave, isn't it?*

"I actually wouldn't care," I lied. "You can if you like."

His eyebrows rose halfway up his forehead.

"We're just friends, M. Why would that bother you?" I goaded him a little further with a hint of a smile, daring him to suggest otherwise.

He was quiet for a couple seconds. "I just don't need to see that shit."

A few days later, we were perched on a railing in City Centre mall sharing pretzels before heading to the movies. I looked at him and said, with a glint in my eye, "You know, you're kind of like my platonic boyfriend."

His smile disappeared and he raised his eyebrows. "What do you mean by 'platonic'?"

"You know, like intimate but without the sex. It's kind of nice."

"Haha, I guess so."

"Come on, we should get going if we're gonna make this film." I cheersed the last bit of my pretzel against his before finishing it off.

Things between us shifted after M's twenty-fifth birthday

in November. I planned a whole evening for us. I picked him up from work and we went to one of my favourite restaurants on Whyte Avenue called Chianti. We laughed, ate pasta, and then walked to Block 1912 for dessert.

"You know, I always dread my birthday," he said, "but this one isn't too bad."

"Glad to hear it, M."

We exchanged bites of panna cotta and German chocolate cake, and then hopped back into my car so he could open the presents I'd gotten for him in private. We parked in front of his place and he unwrapped a small Dr. Seuss book called *What Was I Scared Of?*, a black tourmaline stone to help with his sleep paralysis, a moonstone to help with his insomnia, and a custom-made T-shirt with a fake Supreme logo that said *Cortisol,* a word he often used when feeling stressed. I gave him a handmade card with a platypus on it because he once told me he loved them. He read it and his eyes got all watery. He pulled me in for a hug, and we embraced for a while longer than was normal for us.

He pulled away and looked at me. "This is the nicest thing anyone has ever done for me. Love you, Chy." He kissed my cheek.

"Happy birthday, M. I hope tonight made you hate them a little less."

"Good night, Chy." He got out of the car and I drove home.

Some days, I wish we had stayed this way.

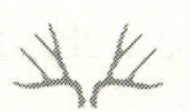

WÎSAHKÊCÂHK was always a trickster, but now, with fox eyes, games were all he wanted to play. All the animals ran and hid from Wîsahkêcâhk because they didn't want to fall victim to another one of his ploys—they were tired of them.

Wîsahkêcâhk was struck with a brilliant idea when he saw Grizzly Bear taking a nap under a tree, berry stains mottling his fur. For miles, every berry patch had been picked clean, leaving none for the rest of the animals and none for the ancestors. Everyone knew never to take all the berries from a single patch, but Grizzly Bear had ignored this lesson because his appetite was insatiable.

Wîsahkêcâhk decided to teach Grizzly Bear a lesson. So, Wîsahkêcâhk dug a pit and transformed himself into a berry patch, and then he waited and waited for Grizzly Bear to wake up.

As soon as Grizzly Bear awoke, he smelled the berries, because after all, blueberries were his favourite. Following his nose, he crept up on the bush with the most decadent aroma he had ever smelled. Without missing a beat, he plucked two perfectly plump berries and popped them in his mouth. Before Grizzly Bear realized what was happening, Wîsahkêcâhk had transformed back into himself and was standing in front of him. Grizzly Bear stumbled back into the pit, crying out in anger. Wîsahkêcâhk cried out too, because those two blueberries Grizzly Bear had plucked were Wîsahkêcâhk's fox eyes, and his sockets now bled and bled.

"Wîsahkêcâhk, how could you do this to me?!" cried Grizzly Bear. "You need to help me get out of here!"

Even though Wîsahkêcâhk was in pain, without the fox eyes, he had more compassion in his heart. "Grizzly Bear, you have been eating too many berries and it's not good for the land. I want to let you out, but you have to promise that you won't pick every berry from each patch!"

"Oh, Wîsahkêcâhk, I promise! Please, I have learned my lesson and I will leave some berries from now on."

So Wîsahkêcâhk let Grizzly Bear out, but Wîsahkêcâhk was still in a lot of pain, and not just from the loss of his eyes. Without the fox eyes, all the tricks he had done were flashing in his mind. Wîsahkêcâhk needed to walk, cry, and feel all the pain from those deeds before he could forgive himself and move forward.

PAHKIPESTÂW is a slight, gentle rain at the start of a storm, and isn't there something so lovely about that? Isn't there always something that entices you to wander outside your home and find yourself under that gentle beginning?

A couple days after M's birthday, we had a shift together and I was having a bad day. As I was leaving the gym, I went to say goodbye to him. He was standing in the middle of the heavy-weight lifting area. He took one look at me and said, "Is everything okay?"

I started crying. He pulled me in for a hug in the middle of peak gym time, without caring who saw or what assumptions they made.

I spoke through soft tears. "I'm just so overwhelmed with everything, M. I'm trying my absolute best. I'm working full time to pay all my bills, I have three essays due, and everything feels like it's piling down on top of me."

He hugged me again and said, "I'm sorry, Chy. You got this. You're going to do great things one day—you already are. Can we hang out tomorrow? I'll come to your place and we can make dinner together. I want to talk to you about something and I think it might make you feel a little better." His eyes were liquid amber.

"Yeah, sure. We can do that." I was so curious that it stopped my tears.

The next night, M came over.

I was sitting on my mattress in the living room, where I had nestled it in front of my small sectional and covered it in a million pillows and soft blankets. I had been sleeping in my living room for weeks, the four walls of my bedroom caving in on me at night, exacerbating my sleep issues. It was cozier to have my mattress in front of my TV so Rick and Morty could lull me to sleep.

It reminded me of childhood. When my parents were together, we would drag a mattress into the living room, cover it in blankets and pillows, and have epic movie nights with snacks and laughter. After they split up and Frank went to prison, I still did this with my mom and sisters. Some of my favourite memories are of nights spent on mattresses in living rooms. It was comfortable. It was childhood.

M set his gym bag on the ground and sat down next to me. "So, I've been thinking about us a lot," he began. "The other day Matt came into my office and he was like, 'Yo, tell me you're still hitting that,' and then he nodded over to where you were working out."

"Ugh, why'd he have to say it all gross like that?" I shook my head, the corners of my mouth curling into a frown.

"Yeah, I don't know. I kind of wanted to hit him for it. And then I have to see Mitch coming up to the front desk all the time and obviously flirting with you. I saw him that one day, like, massaging your shoulders, and I was so fucking pissed."

I just listened.

"It kind of just, like, really hit me when you told me that I was your platonic boyfriend... I ended things with Annie and want to focus on you. You treat me so well, Chyana, and I think that I can make you happy. You've been so stressed with school and work and you're always hustling. I notice. I want to be there for you."

I was shocked.

"I guess what I'm asking, or proposing, and in no way do I want you to feel pressured to say yes... but would you want to be in an open relationship?"

My heart fluttered. "An open relationship... How exactly would we make that work?" It seemed like a logical solution. It could allow us to be together, be happy, but without provoking the anxiety I experienced when trying to trust my romantic partners. I wanted to try it, for me and for him.

We stayed up the whole night and figured out the rules and limits. We were making the perfect plan for *us*—figuring out a way to be together that worked for both of our commitment issues.

M's greatest flaw was his anger.

There were times when he came up to the front desk after a guy had been talking to me for a moment longer than he liked and he would pace back and forth, making accusations, nostrils flared. He would storm away, and then come back, honey in his eyes, and apologize. Then we would run off to the staff room and fuck and everything would be better.

And then there was the time he saw our co-worker Mitch harmlessly speaking with me at the front desk. I heard the clicking and clacking of M's dress shoes before he appeared; I always knew when he was approaching. "Why the fuck are you always up here?" he demanded. "Don't you have some people to train or something to do other than just stand here?" I sat in my chair, frozen and embarrassed, and later had to sit through a lunch with Mitch telling me how I could do so much better. I knew full well I wasn't going to leave M.

It's hard to leave when you want someone, something, so badly.

My greatest flaw was my inability to trust any man close to me. When I tried to love someone it was like we were sandpaper rubbing against each other. An uncomfortable push and pull of talking myself off ledges.

There was the time M told me he wanted to get a friendly dinner with Annie and I berated him. He left to go for dinner with his family and I sat on my phone, stalking every photo of this girl, obsessing, comparing, deciding that I was less cool, less pretty, less worthy of his love and attention. Every "like" he had put on her pictures made my blood boil, and when I saw that she could deadlift heavier than me, any semblance of self-worth or delusion of superiority I'd had was deflated and I sat there and cried. After his family dinner M told me that his brother had said he was an idiot for even asking to go for dinner with Annie and that I had every right to feel uncomfortable. M admired his brother above anyone else.

I would peek my head around the front desk and look into the gym to see if he was talking to any girls. Sometimes he was and sometimes he wasn't, but every time, I grated my agitated words into him. When he sat next to me on my couch, I watched his screen, memorized his phone passcode, and then would snoop through his texts and photos when he was asleep beside me. Sometimes I found nothing, but when you're looking for something, you will eventually find something. That was how I discovered he still had nude photos of other girls on his phone. I lost it and screamed at him.

"What the fuck is the point of an open relationship then?" he spewed at me.

"I just don't want mine next to theirs. It makes me feel like I'm on the same level as those girls."

But it was more than that. I didn't want there to be any photos of other women on his phone at all.

It was then that he admitted to snooping through my laptop and seeing intimate photos and videos of me with my ex-boyfriends, so wasn't I such a hypocrite? But my reasons were superior to his because these were men I used to love, and those girls were nothing more than a spank bank.

"I never look at them, M," I assured him.

"Neither do I."

"Well, let's just both delete them, then." It was always a fight before we could ever talk reasonably, but then we would be tender and he would be inside me again. We cooked dinner and cuddled while watching movies. He started calling me his koala. I called him Grizz because he was like a giant grizzly bear, ferocious at times but also soft, delicately kissing my shoulder behind closed doors.

Our open relationship became increasingly volatile, and each time we made up, I felt closer to him, cared for him more. I cared too much for him to not be bothered seeing him flirt with random girls at the gym, to not care about photos. We would fight, argue, blow up, make up, and I was going insane. I hated him and loved him.

Red flags are easier to spot and easier to leave in the beginning.

They look different in the thick of it.

One day I was alone at his apartment, waiting for him to get back from lacrosse practice. His laptop was on the bed, and I logged in. I found out that he had saved all the nude photos of those girls. He'd never deleted them. Not even after I had deleted all the photos of my exes. I vibrated with anger. I knew right then and there that I did not want to be in an open relationship. The comfort of the open relationship was supposed to be based on honesty, freedom to do whatever with whomever, but we were both failing at this illusion.

I ended it. I didn't scream or yell; I just simply told him that what we had set out to do wasn't working.

He was lying and I was miserable.

KASÎSÎKWAHK is when it is raining hailstones, and sometimes in Alberta the hail gets so big that it dents cars and homes, and people have to run for shelter under concrete car parks. There is something fun and thrilling about those escape runs, and once, M and I ran through the streets of downtown Edmonton from hail the size of golf balls.

After I ended our open relationship, M suggested the last thing I expected—that we close our relationship. Just him and me.

"Are you sure you're capable of doing that?" I asked.

"Yes... I think I can. I have never cared about someone as much as I care about you, and I don't want to lose you."

It's what I had wanted the whole time. For him to want to be with just me. For me to be enough. I desperately wanted to be worthy of being loved.

I was in the third year of my undergrad, and that April I planned to go for a semester abroad in Italy, the one place I had been dreaming of going to since I was eighteen. We decided that once I left, we would part ways.

We wanted to enjoy our time together before it came to an end. We should have known it would blow up in our faces. I had compromised myself to be in an open relationship, and now M was compromising himself to be in a closed one. We tried to be more like each other because we were addicted to spending time together, but we already had our patterns. I would yell and cry, and he would yell louder and cry softer. I'd have a bad day, my dad's birthday, lying on the floor, malnourished, staring at the ceiling, eyes red, swollen, and he would come over and cook me pancakes, playfully forcing me to lick syrup off a spoon, kissing my thigh and pulling me in close. *You're going to be okay, Chy.* We'd toss a lemon back and forth at two in the morning in my living room and we'd laugh, our sadness melting away. When I was on my period he brought me cookies and a rose and ran to the store in the middle of the night for tampons. I would run him Himalayan salt baths, caress his back to help him fall asleep, and be his big spoon, even though he was so much bigger than me. We were living-room slumber parties, outdoor workouts, after-work donairs, and late-night conversations.

But it wasn't fun when we were sitting at the front desk at work on a slow Saturday and I saw a Tinder message pop up at the top of his phone and he claimed it was an old one. It wasn't fun when I asked him to show it to me and he quickly deleted it. It wasn't fun when I told him to leave me alone and he stormed away only to storm back and pace back and forth in front of the desk telling me how he had fucked up. It wasn't fun to vibrate with anger, and then watch him vibrate with something darker, a glimpse of that place he would sometimes go and I had to learn how to bring him back from. It wasn't fun when I forgave him and gave him a little more of me, again, losing a bit of my light each time. It wasn't fun when I looked in his phone and saw that he had been sexting some girl, asking her to come over the one night he spent away from me. It wasn't fun when I shoved him awake and threw all his things into his bag and told him to get the fuck out of my apartment. It wasn't fun when he didn't listen and instead followed me around, the same way the Charismatic Sociopath had, and I smashed my candles, a plate, and my Polaroid camera. I picked up the mattress from the living room floor as if it weighed five pounds and carried it back into the bedroom while he kept following me. And it wasn't fun when he grabbed me by the arms and tried to calm me down, assuring me she didn't come over and telling me he didn't know why he did it. I was leaving so soon and *Why the fuck couldn't you just wait another week?* It wasn't fun when I punched him in the arm and told him he needed to let me go and leave now because I was scared of the anger I was feeling.

It wasn't fun when I watched him walk out my door, defeated.

I cleaned up my apartment with blurry eyes.

He called later that day and apologized, telling me he understood if I never wanted to speak to him again, but then he said the one thing he knew would pull me back in.

He told me he was in love with me and he just didn't know how to deal with that.

I felt everything, and he ran away each time he felt anything. The classic love story between the anxious and the disorganized.

"It's probably too late, isn't it?" he said.

I hated myself for the power he held over me.

I hated myself for getting pulled back in.

I hated that I let him take me for gelato. I hated myself so much for wanting to believe his promise to be better, for choosing to believe. I hated myself for wanting that last week with him. I hated myself for the horrible things we did to each other, said to each other, and then excused because of the shitty things we had gone through as children.

I will never forget the worst day we had. I had just finished packing up my apartment, storing my things at my mother's place, and I would be living with M during my last week in Edmonton before leaving for Italy. I was sitting on my bare apartment floor and hacked into his Instagram account. I wanted to see if he'd stopped messaging that girl but instead saw that he was on Tinder and had been asking other girls for photos. I called him and said that I was done and would stay with my mom for my last week in the city. *You're always fucking invading my privacy and that's the same fucking shit that my mom used to do. What the fuck?* He screamed that he wished he was dead, hung up the phone, and didn't answer when I called back. I drove to his place and found his phone on the bed, but he was nowhere to be found. I panicked.

I made myself small and sat on the smallest corner of his bed. I was in his bedroom when he came back. *M, please. I'm sorry. I didn't mean to trigger all of this. Please.* His nostrils flared and his pale, thin lips sputtered. *It's your fault. You've done this to me. I hate my father, and here I am becoming him. Fuck. Fuck you. You fucking—*

He picked up a sweater that was next to me on the bed and ripped it apart, scattering his rage across the room. He picked up his lacrosse stick, raising, smashing, and pacing. He moved on to the laundry hamper and smashed it. A dresser. A candle holder. Flying bits of plastic and glass cut past my face, through my hair, in between my legs. I covered my face and crumpled as small as I could. *Be small. Be calm.* He raised his stick to the TV. *M, no.* He stopped, shoulders rising and falling in great peaks. He left with his lacrosse stick and his lacrosse bag and I stayed.

There were no tears for this moment, just brooms. I cleaned up. I bought a new candle and lit it. I wiped the surfaces. I sat. I waited. When the stars came out, he came back, walked over to the bed, crawled above me, wrapped his arms around me, nuzzled into my neck, kissed it, and whispered, *I'm sorry.* I told him, *It's okay.*

My body was the sky and he splattered it with stars, but everyone else only saw the daylight. I looked different at night.

He fell asleep in the nook of my neck.

I lay awake for hours.

The next day we went for a walk. He was sweet, held my hand, kissed it. It was grey outside, as it mostly is in April, with the precipice of rain in each cloud. We strolled through his tree-lined neighbourhood off Whyte Avenue, talking about how things needed to be different. *Me leaving will be good for us. I don't want to be this way anymore.*

My last week was almost perfect. He was loving, a cuddly grizzly bear, kissing the top of my head, my cheek, my collarbone. We went for dinner at DaDeO's and shared sweet potato fries and mussels. He kissed my feet after I got a pedicure and said I had the cutest toes in the world. We watched *Back to the Future* and fell asleep tenderly in each other's arms each night, switching between big and little spoon until our alarms rang in the morning.

But the day before I was leaving for Italy, I was dropping him off at a party and crying so hard I could barely see the road. I smashed my water bottle against the steering wheel and threw it out the window. I was screaming through my tears, saying I don't know what. I was so hurt that he didn't want to spend our final night together, and hurt and anger went hand in hand for me then, just like they had for my father. He tried to calm me down, saying he would meet me at his apartment in a few hours. He came back, nestled in next to me, and we stayed up the whole night. In the morning I gave him a letter and made him promise he wouldn't open it until I was already in Italy.

Italy wasn't any better, even though we were no longer technically together, but technicalities are never grounded in honest emotions.

I had just gotten back to the Airbnb after a beautiful day spent in Vernazza, drinking wine on the rocky shore, eating tiramisu, and wandering the cobblestone streets. It was almost two in the morning when M called me. He told me he had hacked into my Instagram and seen messages between me and some guy I met in Italy and accused me of fucking him. I told him that I had seen the messages he sent to a member at the gym who was supposed to be "off-limits." I knew that technically I shouldn't have been mad, but this was after two bottles of wine. We yelled at each other until I finally hung up at four in the morning. He called back over and over, until I finally shut my phone off and fell asleep. We didn't speak for the rest of the trip.

Even so, Italy was life-changing. I made friends, saw new parts of the world. I met a professor who offered me a job as her research assistant for the University of Alberta Prison Project. I jumped off a cliff into the Tyrrhenian Sea on the Amalfi Coast. I drank wine in Orvieto and almost got trapped in the town when the gondola closed. I hitched a ride with a local down to the train platform and made the train with one minute to spare. I drank until four in the morning and woke up at seven and took the train to the next town and got a tattoo. I ate gelato every night under lavender skies overlooking vineyard fields. I ate pici truffle pasta and sang "Vienna" by Billy Joel at a bar. I sat at the front of a boat headed to the island of Capri, jumped off it, and was surrounded by dozens of tiny jellyfish. I wandered the streets of Napoli and ate pizza at the oldest pizzeria in the world. I packed all my things, kissed my new friends goodbye at the airport, and headed back to Edmonton.

Back to work at the gym, back to M.

We fell right back into the same pattern. Blow jobs in the staff changing room, fucking in the executive locker room after close, loving, hating, making up, becoming more dependent on each other. It didn't take long before we were together every day again.

I drove to his house after he said he was going to kill himself and found him lethargic in his backyard, staring at the fence. I understood his depression and he understood mine, but the truth is that two depressed people don't make a right and we brought out the worst in each other.

A slight turn of the head and a breath of *Hi* was how he acknowledged my presence. I sat down next to him, danced a toy bear along his leg in the hope it would crack his mood. I lay down next to him, felt the warmth of the sun, playing different scenarios in my mind for how I could bring him back from that faraway place.

I sat up. "Do you want to pretend to be an animal and I guess what it is?"

"No."

I lay down again. He craved aloneness because it was how he kept himself safe. It's how he always kept himself safe. I knew that well. He hadn't eaten, so I got out of the sun's glare, went to the barbeque, and said, "Does this thing work? I'm going to go to the store and make some food." I knew his meat-perfecting barbeque soul would never let me cook on that thing by myself. I went to grab my purse from the house, and he followed me in. He said he'd come with me, and slowly but surely the darkness in his eyes faded away.

"We're in dangerous waters," he said.

We only held each other tighter.

The thread connecting us was thinner, more delicate, more ready to be severed.

I wish I could say I was better than him, but I wasn't.

I was panicked and pathetic, desperate and addicted, and he was the one to cut it off. I still carry that shame and guilt.

It was hard but necessary for me to look at myself in the mirror and acknowledge that I didn't love myself. If I had, I wouldn't have tolerated or done all that I did.

We never got back together after that, but we were tender in the end. He called me Koala and I called him Grizz and we agreed that we brought out the worst in each other.

The last time I saw him he was leaving my apartment, carrying the things he had left at mine, and I had just gathered the things I had left at his.

He was waiting for the elevator, and I said, "Not even a hug goodbye?"

He said, "You never asked for one," and hopped into the elevator.

After him, I knew I needed to be alone.

I never wanted to be that dependent on another human being ever again.

After him, I had to rebuild my self-worth.

WÎSAHKÊCÂHK cried and wandered for what felt like an eternity until he found a cedar tree to fall asleep beneath. He slipped into a slumber, and before he knew it, he was deep in the dreamworld.

He was being guided through a field by a small monkey, which was strange because Wîsahkêcâhk didn't often cross the ocean. Monkey was happy, jubilant, and filled with so much energy. He kept urging Wîsahkêcâhk forward until they were in a field of sunflowers. Together, they lay among the flowers, watching the clouds in the blue sky above.

"Wîsahkêcâhk, wake up," Monkey told him. "I think all your tears have finally dried up."

Wîsahkêcâhk realized he could see Monkey, he could see the sky, he could see the clouds, he could see the sunflowers, and he could feel all the beauty—all the love.

He woke up under the cedar tree and blinked a couple of times. After all his crying, the sap that was covering his eyes had been cleared away. Wîsahkêcâhk could finally see the world again—all the good, and all the bad.

He looked beside him, and sitting among the leaves was a perfect sunflower.

Wîsahkêcâhk rubbed his eyes, thankful to see clearly, fully, for the first time.

Part IV

Nîswahpitam

She Ties Bones Together as Two

ATI-MÊSTITÊW is when it is boiling away, it is boiling low, it is starting to evaporate, and I suppose that's what this whole process has been about—boiling my past away, but not the kind of boiling that is violent or makes a thing disappear; the kind that is gentle, the kind that is a transformation.

After graduating from the University of Alberta, I drove across the country and stood at the front door of my new apartment in London, Ontario. It was the biggest place I had ever lived in. I noticed each stride that brought me from the front door into the hallway, past the living room, by the dining room, into my bedroom, and then across and into my office—with my wooden desk, the biggest I had ever owned, my fancy computer, and then my bookshelf lined with books. I took a deep breath. Movement. True movement. I marvelled at the solitude, the courage. I felt gratitude for the space, time, and energy to begin writing my story.

Our story.

I sat down and wept.

I stood up and made my way through the dining room.

It took me weeks to resist the urge to run from room to room. I had always lived in small places filled with my mother's knick-knacks, my sisters, and our friends. Space was always occupied, and now there was so much that was free, vacant. But not a sad vacancy, or the freedom of a forest. It was more like a clearing, room intentionally made and waiting to be filled—blank pages waiting.

In the dining room I found the reading nook and saw my drum leaning against the wall—the one I had made when I was fourteen. I remembered the woman with deep brown skin who wailed the loudest cry I had ever heard, and now I understood the weight of all she carried that needed to be released. I brought the drum to my nose and inhaled deeply. I pictured a deer bending its head to graze dewed grass early in the morning. I watched the deer through voyeuristic eyes, imagining my father behind the scope: his muted breaths, contained within his chest, inaudible to the ears of the prey—the weight on his shoulders as he pressed down on the trigger, slightly, pausing to appreciate the beauty of the animal within his sight. CRACK. The deer fell down.

I made my way back to my office and sat down at my desk.

It was time.

Creative writing allowed me to work through and express the trauma that defined my childhood. When Frank was incarcerated, I locked myself in my bedroom and wrote. I wrote him letters that I never sent, poems I never shared, and stories with alternate endings. Writing is catharsis and it is the most powerful tool I have used on my healing journey.

I wrote each morning, day in and day out. I cried. I started eye movement desensitization and reprocessing (EMDR) therapy and wrote throughout. I told my therapist that sometimes I don't know where my anxiety comes from. It just emerges. She told me to pay attention to the moments I got the worst anxiety.

For a long time I was scared to answer the door. My heart raced if I didn't get a forewarning from a family member or friend announcing they had arrived. My vision blurred and I forgot to breathe.

Breathe.

I held onto walls and took deep breaths until I was sure I would no longer fall.

So much of my childhood was spent waiting behind closed doors.

Waiting in a corner.

Waiting in a locked bedroom.

Waiting outside a locked bedroom.

Waiting inside a front door with all the locks engaged and a knife in my hand.

For a long time, and even now sometimes, there was a discomfort in the way memories held themselves in my stomach. If you've ever laid out a blanket flat and pinched the centre, beginning to spin it, watching as it acts like a black hole, sucking up the rest of the blanket—traumatic memory is much the same.

My therapist was in my ear, telling me to hold on to myself and to use one of our EMDR techniques: finger tapping. We began with a difficult memory and started to tap the eyebrow area, beside the eye, under the eye, under the nose, the chin, the beginning of the collarbone, and under the arm. I had to tap out those memories, and then the brain would think of them differently. The body won't hold on to them the same way: internally, we begin to release them. That's what she said.

In one session I sat on a couch and held on to two small oval devices and closed my eyes. I felt them alternate vibrations in my hands as I thought of a memory.

The house was dimly lit with old lamps emitting a soft yellow glow. I sat on a hand-me-down sofa. I got up and stared out the window. I was probably nine. There was quiet behind a closed door when there should have been some splashing. My breath quickened.

He'd been in there for more than an hour. *What could be happening?*

An hour earlier my dad had come home, his large frame stumbling through the doorway. He threw some money on the coffee table and grunted, "Order some pizza."

I looked up at his lazy eyes, drooping low as if the floor were pulling them down. He swayed from side to side. *Parents have pink eyes because when they grow up they lose the whiteness of their youth.* He smelled like the bottom of a Tylenol bottle. "I'm gonna have a bath," he said, and disappeared behind the closed door.

I got up and slinked down the long linoleum hallway, a subtle glow pouring out from under the door as I pressed my ear against it. It was silent. I knocked softly.

"Dad?"

Nothing.

I knocked louder. "Dad, are you okay?"

Still nothing.

I banged. "Dad?! Open the door!"

But it stayed shut.

I went to my bedroom and grabbed a bobby pin from on top of my dresser. I pulled the two metal prongs apart and ran back to the bathroom door. I stuck the pin inside the lock until I felt it press against something small that released under the pressure. I opened the door.

He was naked and asleep in the bathtub. His mouth was under the water as his head lolled downward, his nose millimetres from submersion. Sobbing uncontrollably, I reached my lanky arms into the water, pulled his head up, and shook him until eventually he woke up.

"Sorry, my girl. Dad was just tired."

My therapist brought me back to my happy place, and then I came back to the room.

"How was that for you?"

There was discomfort in my stomach, but when she asked me to assign that discomfort a number—"On a scale of one to ten, how uncomfortable does that memory feel?"—my answer was now only a four after having been a nine when we began.

In an even earlier memory, I was about six years old. Punished for reasons completely forgotten to me, I stood in a corner and listened to my dad's booming voice echoing in the background. It could've been any corner, away from distractions, away from siblings, away from people. The amount of time I spent in a corner is not something I can recollect, but I stood in many. I wore one of those hair clips that snaps into place. I took it out and began to snap it.

Open, closed, open, closed, open, closed.

I traced a pattern with the metal clip, leaving a pencil-like mark on the white wall. I drew hearts and stars, and attempted to draw a cat before resorting to curved lines that I imagined to be a path. I traced that path all the way to the plug-in socket before inserting the clip inside the outlet. I remember my scream and the way it burned, and I remember my mother pulling me away and yelling at my father. I never stood in that corner again; instead my punishment was to be banished to my bedroom.

Locked doors.

Bedroom doors.

Bathroom doors and me,

locking myself inside as I grew older,

blades pressed into my flesh.

My therapist had been saying something about anxiety, but I must admit I hadn't heard a word. Tapping, ah yes, the tapping. Listening. Must listen to the body.

That is enough for today, good work.

"Same time next week?"

"Yes."

I went home and lay on the floor in my office, hundreds of kilometres away from every person that was comfortable and home to me. I fell in love and pain with myself and the pages and the four walls of that room. All I had space for was those four walls, the round vibrating devices of EMDR, the words, the tears, and every emotion that came flooding out of me after the previous fifteen years of processing, grieving, releasing.

A book was brewing, bubbling out of me, and the only thing I could do was follow the impulse.

I learned what a master of fine arts was from reading the author bio in Terese Marie Mailhot's *Heart Berries*. I applied to six universities because I was afraid I wouldn't get accepted into one. As each acceptance came through, I felt a surge of joy, like I was getting closer to achieving my goals—becoming a creative writing professor and dedicating myself to finishing my book.

I was cooking two over-easy eggs when I saw a New York number calling me.

"Hello?"

"Hi, is this Chyana? This is Wendy Walters calling from Columbia University."

I blacked out after I heard the word *accepted*, chills running up and down my body, shooting out of the crown of my head toward the spirit realm. This was the program I was meant to attend. I could feel it. After I got off the phone, I texted my family group chat. I then collapsed on the living room floor and started sobbing. I got up and jumped for joy, jumping in circles all around the living room until I spun myself dizzy.

Years of everything I had been carrying all fell off me at once. *How did I, Chyana Marie Sage, a girl from the hood in Edmonton, Alberta, daughter of a drug dealer, make it to where I am now?* It was time to start packing, because the rest of my life was about to begin.

IN 1883, Sir John A. Macdonald, first prime minister of Canada, told the House of Commons: "When the school is on the reserve the child lives with its parents, who are savages; he is surrounded by savages, and though he may learn to read and write his habits, and training and mode of thought are Indian. He is simply a savage who can read and write. It has been strongly pressed on myself, as the head of the Department, that the Indian children should be withdrawn as much as possible from parental influence, and the only way to do that would be to put them in central training industrial schools where they will acquire the habits and modes of thought of white men."

NAMATAKOW means he disappears, he is gone, like when you place a glass of water in the sun and, as the earth rotates, the water slowly evaporates until it has dried up completely. The sun is like that, powerful enough to pull anything toward it.

The summer after Frank went to the Edmonton Remand

Centre to await his trial, we were waiting for our new placement with Métis Urban Housing. We changed our phone numbers and waited to begin a new life, free from the threat of Frank finding us once he was released. The days and time pulled, evaporating his essence. Evaporating the father from my life until there was a vacancy there, a hole that needed to be filled.

I was floating in a fog, a passenger on an invisible mechanism that carried me through the motions of each day. My life with my father, and the time immediately following it, often feels like a distant dream, a fable, my own personal Brothers Grimm fairy tale encapsulating all the forebodings and words unspoken in "The Girl without Hands"—the story where a daughter is unknowingly sold to the devil by her own father. When given the opportunity to go in her place, the father refuses, and instead chops off his daughter's hands to ultimately save himself. In the end, the daughter miraculously gets her flesh-and-blood hands back, and I need to believe that is representative of the ways that trauma inflicted can be healed.

In therapy I learned that perpetrators have ways of telling on themselves. They give us small indicators of the wrongs they are doing. Frank's tells were quite obvious in retrospect. He often warned me to keep my eyes open for the bad men in this world because they were everywhere. He warned me about an uncle who was accused of touching a young girl. He warned me about the young guys in my classes, my friends, and told me not to be afraid of kicking them in the nuts as hard as I could. If, from his car, he saw me hanging out with male friends, he would unroll his window and stare them down, threatening them with only a glance not to touch his little girl. He sparred with me, taught me how to defend myself, tested my reflexes for how quickly I could duck, weave, and evade. He warned me that pedophiles and rapists were everywhere and not to trust any strangers, but also to be wary of the people I knew. He told me never to trust any of his friends, but especially not to trust men.

When I was thirteen years old, I wrote this letter and never sent it:

Hey Daddy,

I feel so sad and depressed and all I ever wanted was to grow up with you right there beside me. I was your little girl and you were my daddy bear, my protector, the one man in my life who would always be there. If you think this is easy for me, it's not. In my perfect world you would be my dad and Orleane and Chayla would be right there with me and mom would be truly happy again. Orleane would be a happy person and not so shy. It kills me more than anything and no one could understand. My first word was dad and I never thought someone so special that they took my first word would forever take that away from me. You were my best friend, my father and protector. At one time I would choose you over anyone, but now it's the complete opposite of that. I'm always going to love you no matter how much I wanna forget about you. It's killing me to not just shoot everyone in the way of you, just to hug you, and for you to be my daddy bear again. But that is forever gone. I no longer have you as my friend or daddy or protection. Now men can hurt me, take advantage of that spot of love I crave for a dad. It's now wanting to get any male to love me unconditionally when that should have been your job to make sure no man hurts me, and to walk me down the aisle when I'm getting married. Now who did you resign your job to? Anyone? 'Cause that's what you did. You gave me away to any man who could fool me. But I was fooled by you, Daddy Bear, only because you fooled yourself and got in too deep in your own manipulative and destructive ways. Growing up you taught me to keep my guard up with boys. You told me about the bad people, although I didn't know you were warning me about you. A long time ago you told me that Orleane, Chayla, and me were your world, that you would die without us. So why would you take yourself away from us? I never wanted this. I wanted you to be there for me whenever I needed you or cried for you. Now I can cry for hours on end with no daddy coming to my rescue. I was always the one to get through to you. Did you block out every word I said to you with your horrifying thoughts? I just wanna be able to be happy again, to be able to find myself. I have no idea who I am anymore. I want to be free from this misery. I'm going to come and visit you one day, tell you all I need to say. So many words and thoughts run through my mind in one day I couldn't fit them on any amount of paper. Do you know what it's like to hate someone but love them double as much? It's a bitch. You lose focus of everything you had coming to you. People say I have a lot of potential to be a model, but now I'm so lost in life I can't even do anything normal. I smoke weed almost every day, sometimes three to six times a day. The first summer after everything happened, I went on binges with ecstasy. That went on until right before my thirteenth birthday. I smartened up though. I still smoke weed. I still drink. I'll get back to you when I'm doing good.

Bye.

Thirteen years old is such a precious time in a young person's life. It's a time when we're making sense of our new body, the changes that are ongoing, and making space for the new person we're morphing into. At that age, we don't feel that young, or at least I didn't. At thirteen, I was thinking of the void that existed inside of me without having the love of a father, and the ways I could try to fill it.

The absence of a parent manifests in so many different ways in each child that is forced to grow up without one. But yet, the challenges of growing up with a parent who is unstable, abusive, or unable to care for us in the ways that we need is equally harmful.

I think of the nights I spent at random guys' houses. Orleane and I and our friends would make a game of it, feverishly texting all the guys we knew to find out where the parties were and what people were up to before collectively deciding where to go. We found the men who wanted to get young girls drunk, and we didn't have to look far. One night I disappeared for more than twenty-four hours and my mom called the police, panicked and alarmed until I showed up at the house in the late afternoon. She grounded me for two weeks, banned me from the garage—our weed-smoking den—furious that I didn't call.

The truth about that night is that when I woke up in the morning I didn't have a phone, and I was too young and too scared to ask the guys I was with if I could use their phone. I was only fourteen years old and they were in their twenties, so I lingered for a bit, smoking weed with them until one of them asked me if I needed to call someone for a ride.

Then there was the time when I was twelve years old and stood in a park with Orleane and some of our friends, all under the age of sixteen but feeling full grown.

A green pill rested delicately on my tongue and purified water hurried it down my throat.

It was the first time I ever tried ecstasy.

That happiness, that joy, that exhilarating wave that washed over me was unlike anything I had felt before. Everything was a dream, a good one where you emerge through a set of doors and all you see is the vast ocean before you, white sand, and not a soul around. In those days I was only happy when I slept because getting lost in my dreams was much easier than living as a lost person, living as a girl without a father, living as a girl with a father who was as fucked up as mine was, and ecstasy was like dreaming while wide awake.

I felt the adrenaline rush through me, whip through my senses like when someone pushes one of those metal head massagers down your scalp until the tines reach the nape of your neck. A tiny pill, such great heights, a height I wanted to linger with, dwell on, converse with.

Is this what happiness feels like? Have I ever actually felt happiness?

As we dizzied ourselves running through the park, I realized how thirsty I was. I walked to O'Leary swimming pool with Orleane and our friend Aaron so I could fill up my water bottle while they waited outside for me.

There were four sketchy men standing nearby, watching me.

"Look at her, she's only twelve. Let's go, let's get her."

My heart raced. *How did they know I was twelve? I don't look that young. Everyone always thinks I'm sixteen. What the fuck?* I went to the lady at the cash register and asked if I could use the phone and called Aaron.

"There's these guys in here, I'm really scared. They said they're gonna take me."

"Hold on, I'll wait right outside the door. Come out."

I ran out the door and straight for Aaron and Orleane.

Aaron went inside to check it out.

There was no one there except for a janitor.

Around the corner, I began to dry heave.

I had hallucinated the entire thing. There were no men waiting to kidnap me.

Because of my father's lessons, I became a very sensitive, alert, heightened young girl, and I am still that way to this day. Each car that drives by is a threat. Each man that catcalls me is a kidnapper, and each man that I walk past won't even have the opportunity to come close to me because I cross the street before that moment can arrive, denying them proximity for any kind of opportunity.

Part of me is thankful for those lessons because I have had to run from men in cars a few times: once when I was twelve and once when I was twenty-three. Another time I had to run from a man, and it's fucked up, but if I wasn't still partly that fearful young girl, would I have been alert enough to run in time?

Those three times, I might never have made it home.

But the irony is so rich, so pungent that it assaults my nostrils in the same way I taste iron before my nose bleeds. *It sticks to the back of my throat in the same way, Daddy Bear, because you were warning me about you the whole time.*

INDIGENOUS WOMEN make up 10 percent of the total number of missing women reported in Canada, even though they make up less than 4 percent of the Canadian population. The National Inquiry into Missing and Murdered Indigenous Women and Girls reported that in 1980 Indigenous women accounted for 9 percent of female homicide victims, and in 2014, they accounted for 21 percent of female homicide victims. Today, Native women are twelve times more likely to be murdered or go missing than any other demographic. We are sixteen times more likely to be killed or to disappear than white women.

The red hand painted over the mouth has become the widely recognized symbol of the movement that stands up for missing and murdered Indigenous women and girls. In 2019, the National Inquiry released its final report, issuing 231 calls for justice and action to put an end to the violence. The report gathered data that outlined the main causes across the country for this violence rooted in colonialism, racism, and discrimination, citing issues caused by the Indian Act, the forced relocation of Indigenous people, residential schools, the child welfare system, and the Sixties Scoop.

Throughout my life, so many Native girls I grew up with went missing, and many never made it back home. I always wondered: Why is it that when a white woman goes missing, it's all over the news, our cellphones, AMBER alerts issued everywhere, but when a Native girl goes missing, we barely hear anything about it outside her own family and community members? Rectifying this violence forces all of us to acknowledge the hundreds of years of violence, colonialism, genocide, and mass displacement of Indigenous Peoples across Turtle Island.

I think of those times I had to run from cars, both times driven by white men. One, screaming at me to get into the back, and the other, silent, older, sitting in a white truck, watching me, following me, waiting, but I ran down a one-way that he couldn't turn onto and escaped.

My heart beats for the women who never made it home.

MESCIPAYIW means to evaporate, and what is evaporation if not the process by which a liquid becomes a gas—but that process requires heat to the point where water molecules move and vibrate and dance so quickly that they escape into the atmosphere as vapour. They must escape because the environment becomes too intense for their survival; they have to shift and transform into something else, someplace else, escaping to where they can survive.

During my master's degree at Columbia University, I asked Chayla if she would do an interview with me so I could try to fully understand her perspective on what happened throughout our childhood. The look on her face was one of terror, but acquiescence. She raised her eyebrows and said, "Oh shit, I think I'm gonna be busy... for uh... ever." We laughed nervously.

By the time I was ready to put together her piece of the puzzle, I was living in New York and she was back in Edmonton, being a wonderful mother to my beautiful niece Mckinley and brand-new nephew Madden. We had to wait until late at night, after the babies had gone to bed.

I asked Chayla if her husband, Josh, was going to be around for the interview, and she said yes. "He's here gaming. I would go to the spare room but... it's right next to Kin's room."

"It's normally better if you're totally alone because we tend to be more forthcoming and honest when no one else is around."

"I think we'll be okay. Because there's not a lot he ... haha, well, we'll see."

I heard exactly what Chayla didn't have to say. Sisters are like that; at least, it's the way I am with mine, the way we are with each other: communication through looks and words unspoken. We had a lifetime to perfect it. Chayla was saying that theoretically there is nothing that Josh doesn't know, but she feared that perhaps there was something unaccounted for that might come up, might be a new kind of sensitivity. Chayla grabbed a canned margarita and asked Josh to crack it open for her.

"Shit, should I grab a beverage, too?" I said.

Chayla said instinctively, with emphasis, "Well, *yeah*!"

In certain moments we can still rely on old patterns. Old comforts.

Chayla and I cheersed into our cameras. I could feel that we were both delaying the interview, exchanging mindless pleasantries, but then we both knew it was time.

Some might think that writing about my father would be the most difficult part of this memoir. The truth is that I said goodbye to him when I was twelve years old.

He is like a distant dream.

The hardest parts have been the conversations with my mom and sisters. My tears would come crashing down unannounced and unexpected as an acorn falling from a tree onto my head. Everything I love in this world revolves around my mom and sisters, and the humans they have created.

They are the pinnacle of all my love.

"Tell me a little bit about your life growing up," I began.

Chayla repeated my question before exhaling a long breath, relieved, perhaps, that we were easing in, not diving headfirst into the deep waters in our past.

"A little bit about my life? What the fuck do I say?!"

The first house she remembered living in was the white duplex in Rosslyn on the north side of Edmonton. I realized that the bulk of her memories came from the home where the worst of mine began. I had to force down a lump, an intruder, in my throat.

I always had the memories of the acreage to ground me, those whimsical clips of joy and freedom, wolves and mice, owls and coyotes, salamanders and spools. But if her memories started in the home where I started to harm myself, what did she have to ground her? Where did her stability come from? How was her nervous system affected differently from mine? Our different reactions to our core trauma were reflected in our respective romantic relationships. Hers was a desire to immediately have a family of her own, providing herself with the love she didn't receive, and mine was the opposite—this was the moment I glimpsed a reason why.

Chayla interrupted my reverie by declaring that was a lie. She did remember the acreage. I paused at her choice of word. My mother had also said she lied when she corrected her first memory. Perhaps they both used that word because of our hatred for it. No, we loathe, we deplore, we abominate—we execrate—lies for all the years we had to unravel them in order to make sense of our own lives.

Chayla said she remembered snapshots of images from the acreage: "Snippets of things. I don't have a big, great memory. Just running around all the time with you guys—being outside twenty-four seven. I remember going back to a little pond behind the house. We had to climb a fence to get to it. Dirt gravel roads. I remember walking down a road to see a horse? I just see those images." These were her happiest childhood memories. The lump in my throat lessened at the relief that she could remember the good times we shared as sisters—wild brown children playing in the trees.

The way childhood should have remained.

Before Frank started abusing Orleane.

Before Frank created the divide among us.

Chayla's memories from the duplex on the north side are few and far between, with one big memory: Mom and Frank fighting in the bedroom. Screaming. And then she could hear hitting. Thuds and thumps. Rattles. Voices booming.

"There was one last loud bang, and Mom went quiet. It all went quiet. No more thumps. And then she came out of the room."

Chayla's voice shook and her eyes welled up, speaking the rest through tears.

"She looked ... scary. Beat up. But she was alive, and I was relieved."

Mom rushed over to Chayla, then cleaned herself up in the bathroom and took Chayla out for ice cream.

"I don't think we really talked about what happened. I don't remember."

My eyes watered and chills ran up and down my spine. It was difficult to hear this story from my little sister. She was in kindergarten at the time.

Chayla and my mother both told me their differing memories of this incident.

My memory of the fight that ended our parents' relationship began when I came home from school, walked in the front door, and saw that our living room curtains had been ripped off the wall. The house was in shambles. I called out to my mother and traversed the rubble with my shoes still on and my backpack over my shoulders.

If I asked Frank, how would he remember this moment? Would he remember it at all?

"What are your memories of Frank after that?" I asked Chayla.

Chayla didn't recall much, no loving father-daughter moments. But she recalled a house with a dog that was always locked inside the basement. She has one memory in that house. She was around six years old, alone with Frank and Orleane. They went into the bedroom, leaving Chayla in the living room by herself. The house was quiet, barely a noise audible with the exception of the air escaping the floorboards.

"I felt scared and started banging on the bedroom door." Chayla's voice shook and tears started falling from her eyes. Her banging was met with silence until, finally, Frank answered.

"I didn't know what they were doing or why I was alone or why they wouldn't let me in."

She was afraid, and she feared our father. "He was just a scary guy. He fucking terrified me… That's one of my worst memories. I hate that memory so much because now, knowing—to look back on that memory and know exactly what was happening… I knew something was wrong, but I didn't know what and I didn't know why and I didn't know what to do. I just kept banging."

She let out a big breath and wiped her nose.

I replayed her words over and over again until they no longer felt foreign to my ears. I let them take shape and hold themselves in the depth of my drum.

I was never afraid of my father. Often I was scared *for* him, sitting in stairwells and hallways, flip phone clenched in my palms, heart racing, counting down the seconds until I saw him home safe again. But he did not frighten me, even when I ran away from him down hallways attempting to evade a spanking. It was almost like a game for me. I would test him, intentionally poke at him to elicit a reaction.

I am inching closer to the truth, a truth. It's almost as if we knew two different men, two different fathers. And that must be true for all of us.

The man I knew was open, "honest," raw, and he treated me like an adult.

The man Chayla knew was distant, cold, just out of reach.

The man my mother knew… Perhaps she was the only one who glimpsed enough versions of him over the years to touch on who he actually was—a shapeshifter morphing into many forms.

Orleane... She must have known the darkest, scariest, most haunting form.

Him, no longer a body,

just the bones of a man.

Chayla was so young, so small, yet she felt instinctively that something was horribly wrong. Not knowing what, but knowing.

And banging.

Mistaking small for delicate is dangerous. If you give Chayla lemons and tell her to make lemonade, she'll whip them at a wall and grow her own grapefruit tree in the backyard. Her sadness is a symphony of frogs. In the daytime it's absent, but in the dewy grass under the stars it's the loudest thing you'll hear.

Her small fists pounded on that door, her attempt to stop what was happening on the other side, even though there was no way she possibly could.

I wish I had that strength.

Her little

lemon-whipping,

six-year-old strength.

Chayla had never told any of us that memory before. This was the first time I was listening to my little sister say anything about the things she'd observed. None of us had shared with each other the things that we'd seen, and maybe if we had, things could have changed sooner. But I can't think about those possibilities because I know in my heart that I am the only one who could have changed what happened sooner.

I was the only one at the time who knew the truth; or rather, I knew Frank's truth, and I was his indefatigable minion. To this day it makes me sick to think about.

To this day I look back and think: How on earth did he make me believe that what he was doing was normal?

How on earth, why, why, why... did I keep his secret?

To the bitter fucking end.

After a moment of silence, I told Chayla the story of how Frank told me that he and Orleane were "in love" and going to get married when she turned eighteen. I broke down again, telling her how much guilt I still carried for not saying anything.

"I just thought that was normal, and I have no idea how... To this day, I have no idea how I believed that."

That's when Chayla uttered the words that I knew—that I know—to be true but have had such a difficult time wrapping my head around. "You were a child, though. You were a child. Your parent is supposed to be someone you can trust. Your safe person. You're supposed to be able to trust them, whatever they say... They're teaching you everything in life."

This is my great wound from childhood. Trust. My trust was eviscerated on such a fundamental, intrinsic level during my most formative years, and that has affected most of my relationships ever since. I have struggled to trust anyone who got close to me.

I once joked to my therapist that my brain was wired backward. Most of us learn to trust the people in our lives once we become close to them, grow to love them, but for me, it was the opposite: once I loved someone, I no longer trusted them. If anyone got too close to me, I would hold a magnifying glass to their actions, their words, in search of the ulterior.

I was my own detective novel and you might as well have titled it *Nancy Drew: The Girl Who Will Never Trust.* The ending was simple and took the shape of a self-fulfilling prophecy. If you go digging, you will find something.

And maybe the something is great and severe and protects you from harm, or perhaps it is so menial, so innocuous, but that doesn't even matter because it is enough to make you break your own toe bones and use them as sharp claws to protect yourself in the same way as the Wolverine frog.

I have used those claws against many men who have loved me.

Chayla and I were quiet, until I shared two of my own memories of being on the other side of a locked bedroom door, to show her that she wasn't alone. They were some of the memories I had worked through the most in EMDR.

I was with Frank and Orleane in the basement of the Rosslyn house, before he told me his secret. We were trying to decide on a movie to watch. He decided on *The Amityville Horror,* and then he teased me, telling me how I would be too scared to watch it, so I should go upstairs. He was trying to get me away from Orleane, and it breaks my heart.

In all these memories, Orleane was always quiet, and if she did speak, she would ask me to stay, to not leave her, and perhaps that is why I stayed next to her for most of our lives, even in the moments when I should have left to take care of my own mental health.

I should have been a better little sister.

I should have known that she did not love him back.

I should have known how wrong it was.

She gave me all the clues, and still, it was his voice that I listened to.

I told Chayla about waiting on the other side of another bedroom door that they would disappear behind. No one would answer when I called out, or sometimes he would emerge, give me money, and tell me to go to the store and get some treats. Uncle Jason lived with us in that apartment for months. I've always wondered about the things that might have plagued his heart and mind.

"On some level, Uncle Jason must have known," I said to Chayla. "But Frank was such a charismatic person. He could convince you of anything, make you change your mind. And who the fuck would think that? Especially as young kids, it's not even something that's in your brain to imagine. So who knows what happened between Uncle Jason and Frank."

"Yeah. I can visualize being in the back seat, questioning why Orleane always rode shotgun. And I can envision looking straight ahead, clear as fucking day, going through a drive-thru, and his hand reaches over and goes onto her thigh and her lap. Was that normal? How come he doesn't treat me like that? How come, you know? It's fucked up because we all questioned something at some time." Chayla barely caught a breath before she dove into another memory.

She remembered his handmade cards he sent from jail, a seventh or eighth birthday card in the most beautiful penmanship. He had beautiful handwriting.

"I don't remember much from when he was in jail, but I know how I found out about everything," Chayla said. "I would always fall asleep on the couch, and usually Mom and you guys and whoever else would stay up drinking around the kitchen table and I would just lay there and listen ... and that's literally how I found out ... everything."

"Holy shit. I didn't know that."

"Yeah." She chuckled, a defence against the pain.

"So much of that time is a blur ... Do you remember if we all talked about it together?"

"Mm-mm." She shook her head. "I don't remember you guys saying anything, but you must have ..."

"Well ... I think we all went to Doctor Jim ..." Dr. Jim was the psychologist we saw after we all found out the truth.

"Yeah."

"I don't remember that conversation, if it happened. I don't remember a lot of what came after. I remember drinking a lot. I remember going to court. And then I remember being in the yellow duplex and starting at Kenilworth. It's all ... just a blur."

"Yeah." Her tone was understanding.

"I remember us feeling like we had to protect you ... which I think ... made you feel isolated from us."

"Mm-hmm." Her voice started to shake. "Which I already very much felt. Like beforehand. Before anything ever came out. For my whole life, essentially. I think that's why Mom was so important to me. Because you guys were like"—Chayla was now crying as she spoke—"I know you guys had your own shit, obviously... but Mom was really the only person at times that made me feel loved. But at the same time... for some reason, my emotional needs weren't met. Maybe part of it is because no one talked to me. No one talked to me about anything, ever. So I internalized a lot of shit and worked through all that on my own. Because why would I talk to you guys about it when no one wanted to talk to me? Obviously there's something wrong with talking to others about things. That was Frank's fault, too. Because that was another big relationship in my life where I didn't feel like I was important or loved at all, because I just watched him have a completely different relationship with Orleane, and then you. He gave bribes to both of you, and then I was always left feeling like, well, why the fuck don't I get any of that? I just never understood."

I broke down sobbing at my desk.

All Chayla ever wanted was to be included, acknowledged as a key player in our family—loved. And in the most heightened, fucked-up moment of our lives, we failed her. It was 2006, a time when therapy wasn't normalized, when talking about *anything* wasn't normalized.

It was a time when silence and burial were the socially acceptable modes of dealing with secrets and betrayal.

We failed her because we thought she was too young.

We failed her because we didn't know how to address it.

We failed her because we couldn't even make sense of what had torn our family apart. But perhaps that time shouldn't have been about trying to figure it out. It should have been about being together, connecting, and surrounding ourselves with the comfort of each other, instead of comforting ourselves with drugs and alcohol, activities that Chayla was too young to partake in—activities I was too young to partake in, but did anyway—and that rendered the impossible something possible to discuss.

I remember that summer night after Frank went to jail, during that time when days morphed together, when my mom, Orleane, and I were sitting around the kitchen table drinking and talking about Frank and what had happened.

The unveiling had happened, but still, we were running, not wanting to see, unable to look, unable to sit with ourselves, but passengers, rather, moving through something unspeakable.

So we closed our eyes and drank ourselves to sleep every night.

There were lots of nights when we would sit around the kitchen table drinking two-litres of cider. My aunty Charm, who was both my mother's best friend and Frank's cousin, would often be there with us. Nights filled with cigarette smoke, joints, bottles of vodka, and playing 952 and asshole. Sometimes we cried, sometimes we spoke of our hatred of him—*How could he have done this?*—but we did this after we had put Chayla to bed.

She was still too young: I was only twelve, but she was eight. We tried to shield her from the horror, the darkness, but in our attempt to protect her, we shut her out.

But what exactly did we shut out?

When we shut her out from us, from our drinking, our drugs, we also shut her out from inclusion. Conversations were being had that she should have been a part of, no matter her age, and I wish we had been strong enough so that we didn't need drugs and alcohol to have those conversations. Inclusion and love go hand in hand for a child.

I always thought she needed protection.

We thought she needed protection, but we showed it in all the wrong ways.

She didn't need to be left on the other side of closed doors.

She didn't need to be protected.

She needed to be included.

To me, Chayla is the eye of a hurricane, a calm spot amid a sea of horror. My mom wanted to name her Ocean Pearl. When she was born, I thought she was the smallest thing I had ever seen. I was scared to touch her because I didn't want her to break. She had these moon-filled cheeks that looked as if they would burst if she smiled any bigger, but they never did. As a baby she was so pale, and as she got older, her skin deepened to the same tone as mine. When she began to speak it was with a British accent, and we all knew that she was a special soul who was entering a new life fresh from an old one. Her first words were *french fry*, and she walked around on her small legs demanding popcorn in a British accent.

Now, I can see Chayla, small, delicate, frail, pretending to be asleep on the green couch with the wolf blanket on top of her. I can imagine her shallow breaths, the way she tried to steady them, the way she tried to make herself undetectable, all in the name of understanding her own life, her own father, and why, why, there were still so many secrets being kept from her.

I imagine her there,
alone,
even though we were only a few feet away,
hearing the truth of what happened,
and still lying there,
still pretending to be asleep.

When I think about the gravity of that, the weight that was placed on her, I am struck by what it means to be strong and what it means to be frail.

We were the ones who were too frail to sit her down and tell her the truth.

She was the one who lay there,
ensuring her own truth,
and in her shallow breaths,
pretending to be asleep.

I cannot think of anything that embodies strength more.

THE LACOMBE RESIDENTIAL SCHOOL took my maternal aunty Debbie and her siblings as young children. One of the memories she told me will always stay with me.

There was one little girl in the green dress that I'll always remember. I was never allowed to meet her because she was dark-skinned. The dark-skinned and the light-skinned children were separated. Every chance she got, she ran. If there was a door open... schfeeww, she was out the door. If there was a window open... schfeeww, she was out the window. Just running, like crazy, and you would see these nuns just chasing after her, eh, haha. Everybody was just like, "Go! Go!" hoping she would get away. She never did. They always brought her back. Then we wouldn't see her for a few days and she would show up again in her little green dress. She had such a spirit about her. I often thought I should write a short story about her. The girl in the green dress.

My aunt passed away from cancer a few years after she told me this, but this story lives on inside my memory, the same way Aunty Debbie sitting across from me at her kitchen table while telling it always will too. We can all remember the girl in the green dress, her running, resilient, fighting spirit.

When I think of Chayla and how young she was, so small and fragile, when she heard the fight that ended our parents' relationship, my mind delves back even further to 1996: the year that Chayla was born and the year that the last residential school in Canada closed. I think of our brothers and sisters who attended the schools. I think of my aunts, uncles, and grandparents. I think of the impact on the children who were raised without the nurturing love we all need to develop into healthy, happy, functioning human beings.

I think of their small bodies enduring, witnessing, and enduring some more.

I think of the way those memories have left permanent scars, and then reflect on how those scars are passed down.

I think of the small bodies.

Bodies that never made it home

and turned into bones.

The last residential school closed just two years after I was born, and I think of the way it impinges on my little sister's life, my own, and threatens to take us away. I think of the way the schools and the scoops took all my relatives away, scattered them, and not just physically but mentally, spiritually, and emotionally too.

Studies have shown that children who endure physical or sexual trauma, witnessed violence, or are raised outside of loving, nurturing environments have higher risks of developing negative health issues later in life such as anxiety, depression, heart disease, diabetes, autoimmune diseases, substance abuse issues, and numerous others. In an article in *Health Equity*, Paul J. Kim writes: "Compared to the general population, Indigenous Canadians suffer from disproportionate increases in diabetes, hypertension, substance abuse, mental health concerns, and overall morbidity and mortality in addition to having significantly reduced life expectancy." Research has proven that enduring trauma at a young age leads to these mental and physical health issues later in life, and considering the mass implementation of the scoops and the residential school system, there is no doubt as to why that is.

My mind is filled with ignorant settler discourse that utters over and over and over:

It happened a long time ago.
Can't they just get over it?
How can it still affect them today?
It happened a long time ago.
Can't they just get over it?
How can it still affect them today?

The truth is that 1996 is not long ago, and when I think of the schools, I think of the small bodies. Bodies taken someplace far away from home. Bodies that never made it home and turned into bones.

Bodies that no longer remember a home.

Bodies without homes.

Bodies.

Bones.

Small, fragile bodies that had to endure, had to take on incomprehensible strength, an extraordinary sense of survival, tenacity, resistance, and ferocity just to emerge on the other side whole, or at least something that resembles whole from the outside, and then were sent out into white families or white spaces and expected to wear white faces.

APWEHKASIW is when it is hot enough to sweat, like when you walk outside and stand in the blistering heat of a dry summer day, allowing the sun to warm you so much that it begins to pull the water from within you, speckling your skin with beads of water.

The older I get, the more I want to remember, to juice the past. The more I remember, the more I will understand. Maybe once I understand, I can reconcile every emotion that has lingered beneath my skin and overflowed in the form of alcohol, blood, tears, and sweat. The pain, the loss, the anger, the grief, the depression, the sadness, the betrayal—all are an inextricably woven cord that connects back to a time when I hadn't even inhaled my first breath. Perhaps once I reconcile I can move forward and shed from my brown skin the generations of trauma that have permeated my being. Perhaps I can find the cord and render it healthy.

This is Arthur, a boy who was taken during the Sixties Scoop.

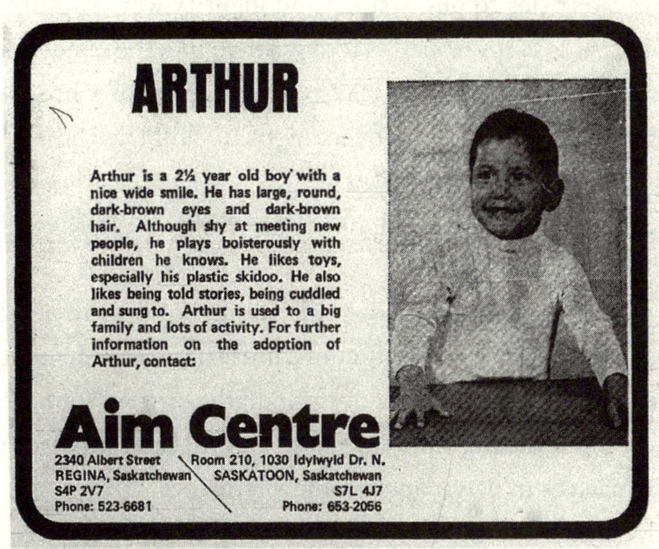

The Sixties Scoop refers to child welfare policies from the 1950s to '80s that forcibly removed more than twenty thousand (the actual number is suspected to be exponentially higher) Indigenous children from their families and placed them in white foster homes and group homes. Often, the children's names were changed so that their relatives couldn't find them. To this day, people are still connecting with their long-lost relatives.

This advertisement is one of thousands placed in newspapers throughout Canada and the US by the Adopt Indian and Métis Project. Program administrators believed that if the children were removed from their homes early enough, they wouldn't "imprint" as Indigenous people. As a result, families were displaced, disrupted, and the tradition of passing down oral history, language, mythology, and legends was severed. When these children were taken away, our ties to our history and identity were ruptured, and that loss reverberates today. Much like the residential school system, the Sixties Scoop was part of a broader plan by the Canadian government to "kill the Indian in the child."

Did they kill the Indian in the child, or did they kill something else entirely?

When I read this ad, see this young boy, I cannot help but think of my family. My aunts, uncles, and grandparents. I cannot help but think of my grandfather, my mosôm, who was taken during this time. Did they all have pictures of themselves in newspapers somewhere, too?

Could I find them? I wonder who did.

I cannot help but think of my father—the disruption in my family.

Was I the groundwater?

Who was the cloud?

Who was the rain?

I knew my father had learned all those stories he told about Wîsahkêcâhk and Witigo from Nimosôm. I hadn't spoken to Frank Logan Sr. since the year of my father's incarceration. So I sent him a message on Facebook and asked if he was willing to share some of our stories with me.

I was sitting at a sports bar and my phone started ringing with a Vancouver number I didn't recognize. The saltwater shores where I was born.

"Tansi!" A big voice bellowed jubilantly on the other end.

I was stunned. "Who is this?" I asked, even though I instinctively knew.

"Mah, it's your grandpa Frank!"

We both started laughing.

"Ahhh, I thought it was you, but I wanted to make sure!" We made small talk for a bit.

"I was thinking," he said. "I don't remember all the stories, but I remember one real good, eh. So I was thinking maybe tomorrow I can tell it to ya. Maybe it's time to tell you about your grandpa's life."

Before we hung up we said, "Love you," and even though this man hadn't been in my life since I was a young girl, nothing felt more natural.

The next day we spoke over Zoom, but his camera was off. I didn't press it and assumed he wasn't ready for that kind of interaction. I left mine on. He asked how I'd been and I told him I was living in New York City, doing graduate school at Columbia.

"It's good to hear that you're moving in the right direction. Following your dreams, your path. Right on."

"Yeah, it's been a journey to get here..."

"No, I can imagine. Jesus Christ, it's been a journey for me to live this long, mah."

We started laughing—the same laugh, one that came from the throat and sounded out each ha-ha-ha.

"Your grandpa only graduated from the school of hard knocks."

We laughed again.

"I remember my dad used to say that."

"Mah! Where do you think he got it from?"

We chatted as if there was never any reason for us to not be in each other's lives. As if there was never a threat of danger in our communication. In the chaos and gut-wrenching pain of my father's incarceration, I had never had the time or mental capacity to grieve the loss of my paternal grandparents. We grieved the ultimate betrayal and loss of our father, but the body and mind can only handle so much. My mother and sisters and I cut off everyone who spoke to my father for fear that he would come after us to take us away from our mother as soon as he was released. I had to say goodbye to my grandparents, who were never anything but loving and wonderful to me. At the time, my body shut down and I didn't have the emotional capacity to even realize how much I missed them.

As I spoke with Frank Sr., I realized how much I had inherited from him. The way he tells stories with humour, seriousness, and sacredness. The way he laughs after his own jokes. The way he talks about the bad shit, and then makes you laugh a moment later. Storytelling runs in my blood, and as much as I want to disavow my father, he will always be a part of me, the way his father is a part of him—the way the three of us can be linked and traced to each other. If you place me next to my father, you will see his cheekbones, his smile that doesn't reach too wide, and his deep brown eyes that light up amber in the sunlight. We have the same shape of face with a nose that tips downward when we smile, and we both inherited it all from my grandfather.

What about the things we don't want to inherit—the bits we want to wash away?

The trauma of the Sixties Scoop and the residential school system continues to affect families generations down the line. Intergenerational trauma can affect anyone and everyone, but Indigenous people across Turtle Island have an intrinsic trauma that affects the entire group. A shared legacy of schools and scoops.

A collective trauma.

A disruption in the lineage.

My grandfather was raised in the Northern Alberta bush, learning to trap, hunt, and live off the land. Everything changed when my kokum, my great-grandmother, packed up her kids and relocated to Edmonton, where they were supposed to live with their father, my great-mosôm—the original Frank Logan. He and his brothers all signed up to fight in World War II, and they all made it back home, physically unharmed. But my grandfather's father abandoned him and his siblings when they were young.

Once the family moved to the city, my grandpa never recalled seeing his dad. The original Frank lived in bars. "Every now and then he would show up, give Mom some money and bring us some goodies," he told me. "I remember this one weekend, a Friday, Mom said go up to the bar and get 'chur dad. He's gonna give us some money. I still remember walking into the lobby, lookin' round, lookin' at this desk and this guy standing behind there. I looked behind him, there was this sign up there, 'No Indians Allowed.' I thought, 'How the hell does Dad get in here?'"

We laughed.

"So I go up to the desk, get him to page Frank Logan. Took about three times before he finally staggered out and said, 'What're you want?'" He chuckled. "'Mom wants some money,' I said. He pulls out some money and says, 'Make sure she gets it.' I said, 'Look at that sign up there, how come you get in?' He says, 'I tell them I'm Scottish.'"

We both laughed at the inside joke. No one can ever guess our heritage and ethnicity. I tell my grandfather the stories of all the times I've been travelling and people have mistaken me for one of their own. It must run in the family.

The original Frank Logan was Chippewa Saulteaux, Scottish, Kahnawake Mohawk, and Irish, and that is just on his paternal side. Both of my great-great-grandmothers, a Kahnawake Mohawk and a Chippewa Saulteaux, shacked up with colonists who adopted the Indigenous way of life. Frank Logan's maternal side is made up of a fierce lineage of Woodland Cree people. My kokum Mary Elizabeth Betty Powder comes from a line of Woodland Cree master women trappers and was the granddaughter of Chief Peeaysis, a Woodland Cree warrior who gave up our Indian Status on that side of the family to fight in the rebellion at Frog Lake. All the Cree women in that lineage are named Mary and Marie, dating all the way back to the early 1800s, which is why I carry a middle name from all those powerhouse Native women.

I think of the letter *M* on my left eyeball. How could I have, for even one second, thought that sign had anything to do with a man? It is my innate physical marker, my clue, my birthright, of these women living within me.

My grandfather has these women in him, too, but he also has the men, his own inheritances. He told me that he was a violent man, and he carried that with him for many years.

"Where do you think that violence came from?" I asked, an impossible question.

He paused before answering. "I would say it came from them ripping us out of our home. I remember that day. I was gettin' ready to go to school. Mom said, 'No, you don't gotta go to school. We got some people coming to talk to us.' Didn't even dawn on me who the hell the ministry was in those days because we never had to deal with 'em back in Fort McMurray. So we were sitting around there, it was about ten o'clock in the morning, and I happened to look out the front window. Squad car pulls up, a black car, a brown car, and another squad car. Thought, 'Holy fuck, what's going on here?' Sure as shit they're all coming into the house. 'Wow, what's happenin'?' Mom went to talk to them, they all come in the house. I can't figure out why they're all here. Mom moved to the side and she started crying—"

My grandfather told the rest of the story through tears.

"The workers told us we were leaving and we had to go somewhere else. Right away the girls started to cry and I'm figuring, 'What the hell they talkin' about we gotta leave? Who the hell are these people?'" My grandfather said a social worker came over and put his hand on his shoulder to take him into the car. "I shrugged him off, told him, 'Don't touch me.'"

The social worker said, "You gotta come with us, that's why the policemen are here."

Grandpa told him, "No, I ain't goin'. This is my home." The next thing he knew a cop rushed over, grabbed him by the arm, and started dragging him away.

"That's when the fight started and they ended up putting me down on the ground. Throwing the cuffs on. I fought 'em all the way. All the way to the squad car. My brother was already in there crying ... We're cryin' ... I look back and I could see one of the workers take Audrey out of Mom's arms ... Mom fell—fell on the steps ... There was nothing I could do to help her." He took a deep breath and released it.

"I would say that's where a lot of my anger started. I carried it for many, many, many years ... too many years.

I don't think I stayed in one place for more than two months. It just wasn't home."

After this story we sat in silence, allowing space for his tears to dry.

My grandfather and his siblings were taken after they moved into the city, where police and child welfare services worked closely together displacing Indigenous children to Euro-Canadian households. My grandfather was born in 1954, and it was in the 1960s that this phase in history accelerated. Indigenous children had been forcibly removed from their homes long before the scoops, but this period accounts for the overrepresentation of Indigenous children in the child welfare system that continues today.

As of 2021, Indigenous children accounted for 7 percent of the youth population of Canada, yet they made up 53 percent of children in foster care, according to Statistics Canada.

When I listened to my grandpa's story, I thought of the young boy in the newspaper. Arthur.

What families found their photographs?

When my grandfather aged out of the child welfare system, he hadn't seen his brothers and sisters in years. The younger ones he hadn't seen for more than twenty years, all scattered with different names in different foster homes with white, often abusive, families.

What happens to the lost children?

What were the repercussions when the government declared stolen children as found children, and advertised missing children as children up for adoption?

Did they kill the Indian in the child, or did they kill something else entirely?

Who is the groundwater?

Who is the cloud?

Who is the rain?

My grandfather had four sons and two daughters. My mother told me that my father and his brothers were raised by the alcoholic, whereas the rest of us knew the sober, funny man. Even though the man I knew was never violent, I know from conversations with my mother that he used to be a different person. My father and uncles were peas in a pod, just like me, Chayla, and Orleane. My dad, the eldest, my uncle Jason and uncle Shane in the middle, and my uncle Justin, the youngest.

Frank was twenty-three years old when he had me, and I can only imagine what had happened in his life in all the years before. Perhaps one day he will be ready to share it with me and I will have one more piece to the puzzle. Now I have lived more life without my father than with him. I am older than he was when he had me and almost as old as he was when he was sentenced for what he did to our family. He served two and a half years, and I know through the grapevine and social media that he has two new children with a girl who is the same age as me and was one of his parents' foster children.

I have two half-siblings I have never met, and I often wonder if they will one day come searching for me—searching for answers, connections, some kind of history that will shed light on their own existence, their own legacy. I know my father is a truck driver and doesn't break the law, but I do not know what kind of father he is to my half-siblings.

Are they his do-over?

During my second Zoom call with my grandfather he had his camera on, and he told me that he and my grandma have custody of Frank's kids, but he visits them on the weekends when he's not working.

Near the end of the call something unexpected happened.

I heard a little girl talking in the background. It was almost lunchtime. Grandpa said he was on a call and Grandma would make her some food. She asked who he was talking to and he told her, "It's Chyana." She said she wanted to meet me, and then he asked me if I wanted to meet her.

I froze in my desk chair. I wanted to see her.

I wanted to hear her voice.

I wanted to know if we shared any features.

Grandpa spun the camera around and in a split second I was staring into the hazel-green eyes of Soarcha. Her face was rounder than mine and reminded me of Aunty Danielle, but she had my dad's wispy curls. My wispy curls that I give round-brush blowouts so as to create more of a separation between my face and his, his hair and mine.

She gave me a shy smile and said hi. I said hello, and then we were both dumbfounded.

"Mah! That's it?" said Grandpa Frank.

After a beat I reminded myself that I knew how to talk to children. After all, I have nieces who are around her age. I shook off my shock and introduced myself, and then asked her how old she was. She was eight.

"What grade are you in?"

"Grade three."

"Do you have a favourite subject?"

"Math." A math girl ... That was good.

"I'm not a math person. I'm terrible at it, so you're probably much better than me. Can you guess how old I am?" I asked her. She couldn't tell, so I told her I was twenty-eight. I'm twenty years older than her. She was quiet.

Grandpa said, "No questions?"

She was still quiet, so I filled the silence by asking her what her favourite colour was. It was pink. She asked me what my favourite colour was. It's purple, and pink, and I showed her my pink water bottle as proof. She told me she had a rainbow room and I told her that was much more interesting than mine, and then it was time for her to run off and eat lunch.

I did not know exactly how I was feeling, but it was not a bad feeling.

I hope Frank is to her the father who lined a flower garden for me with boulders and helped me fill it with soil and plant alpine forget-me-nots.

I hope he is the father who took me into the Northern Alberta bush and taught me how to recognize different animal tracks.

I hope he is the father who baked bannock on Christmas mornings.

After Soarcha ran off, my grandpa told me she's not shy and usually you can't shut her up. He then told me about my half-brother, Steven. He is autistic and was non-verbal for most of his life before my grandparents took legal custody over them. Soarcha used to be his mouthpiece while they were in foster care, speaking for him, anticipating his needs, protecting him, and now she was learning to let him communicate on his own. She didn't have to be his mama anymore.

That little girl had already had to live beyond her years. She was only eight.

Steven is a leap-year baby. When my grandfather told me this my body started vibrating with chills up and down, up and down, up and down ... Steven is my father's son and he is ten.

Naia is Orleane's daughter and she is ten.

Naia was born on February 28, 2012.

Steven was born on February 29, 2012.

A fetus was aborted sixteen years ago.

I cannot even fathom what exactly this means, but it is uncanny.

As my grandfather and I finished our call, he told me about his cousin Roger and how he was always scaring the kids with stories of Witigo. "I remember goin' back to McMurray years ago, when I was a young man, lookin' for him."

He saw their friend Willy and asked him, "Where's Roger?"

"Wah ... Witigo got him."

"What you mean?" he said. "Witigo doesn't exist."

"Well, you gotta see him." Willy replied.

"Where is he?"

"He's usually sittin' in the bar."

So my grandpa went down to one of the oil sands bars. He saw this guy sitting in the corner, huddled there. He had a big parka on, pulled way up, and a toque, pulled way down. My grandpa stared at him; he moved a little closer. "Roger?" He looked much older. Roger's eyes were on fire. "Holy shit, what's a matter with you?"

"Witigo got me," Roger replied.

"Mah, get out of here."

"You better leave me alone," was all he said. The look in his eyes gave my grandpa the chills, so he backed away. On his way out, he saw a friend at the bar and asked him, "What the fuck's with Roger?'"

"I don't know, man, he's fucked up. He went out huntin' one day, was gone for two weeks, which was unusual. He came back and said he was seein' things, talking to people that weren't there."

"Maybe Witigo did get him, I don't know," my grandpa told me. "Never know."

We laughed, but a darkness lingered in both of our eyes.

I thought back to Little Warrior, deep in the boreal forest, and how his middle daughter, Wanderer, had to plunge her strongest arrow through his heart to eviscerate the Witigo.

Frank learned all those stories about Witigo, and Wîsahkêcâhk, from Nimosôm.

I remember when Frank was in my life, before we moved into the city and everything changed. We lived in a trailer on an acreage deep in the Northern Alberta bush with big, tall evergreens framing our property. I was seven and we sat in a circle with the flames at our centre. Looking up, I saw the tips of the trees swaying inward and outward, a little darker than the starlit sky. My two sisters were on either side of me, my mother was across the fire to my right, and Frank was to the left. I looked down at my small feet wearing black combat boots. Looking up from my bare, scarred legs swinging back and forth below the chair, I met the eyes of my dad. He looked back at me and the ember glow illuminated his high cheekbones, casting a shadow under his buffalo eyes.

My buffalo eyes.

The flames spat and crackled at my feet. He opened his mouth and his grave voice told stories of the Witigo, an evil spirit and cannibal who preys on the human soul.

I stood up to wander into the forest to pee. With a smile on his lips, my dad called after me, "Make sure Witigo doesn't come get 'chu."

I wanted to dive further into this memory, but it was blank.

I couldn't remember the specifics of Witigo, or the trickster Wîsahkêcâhk.

As I grew older, I longed to connect with my past, my history. To find that cord and resurrect it. My legacy. Mine, no matter how complicated.

I reached out to Frank to see if he was willing to share stories about his childhood.

My doors are many and locked up, he wrote. *Afraid, I am. Humility, I am terrified! Still my lost soul wanders this space from time to time. Leaving the past seems easier said than done. So, yes, you can send me some questions and I will try and unlock some doors.*

I read his response to a couple of my close friends and they all said he talks like me. They saw a portion of my inheritance.

But what about the things we don't want to inherit?

What about the bits we want to run far away from?

The days carried on, no answers came, and his silence grew louder. But as his silence carried on, I remembered what I said to him when I ran into the forest all those years ago.

"No, Dad. Make sure Witigo doesn't get you."

PÂSTÊW means it dries, it is dried, in warmth, like the earth after a great storm—the soil is drenched deeply, water moving underground until it can't go any farther, and then the sun, with its unwavering power, comes from above, warming the soil, moment by moment, until eventually, the remnants of the storm are no longer, and instead, the water and the sun have worked together, allowing the vegetation to reach higher, toward the sky.

I love Orleane more than anything, and her story is hers alone. And it is different from mine, different from my mother's, different from Chayla's. It is one that is so outside and beyond the scope of what anyone could imagine. I cannot tell you how she felt. I can and will only tell you about her through my eyes. I will tell you what she was like as an older sister. I will tell you all the ways that she has been my best friend, my companion, a pain in my ass, but my partner in crime, and, for my entire life, someone I have tried to protect. I will always protect her.

There is a reason why Orleane comes here, and not earlier. There is a reason why she was the last person I interviewed in my family. There is a reason why every single time I sat down to write about her my insides started to vibrate and I had to run away from my computer. How do I tell her story when I know I could never tell the full story? I don't want to. It is hers to tell when she feels ready to tell it. Protecting her is woven into the fabric of who I am. My love for her is woven into every fibre of my DNA. I could write a whole book about all of our ups and downs, but the truth is that no matter what she does, no matter who she becomes, no matter how she has treated me, how I have treated her, we are both still two girls sitting in a window, vowing to take a bullet for the other.

One of the first things I saw in this world when I opened my eyes as a baby was her smile. Perfectly straight white diamonds decorated half her face. I was lucky because I was born with a best friend who was waiting for me. She was so happy to have me, and her happiness was my happiness as we smeared dandelions on our cheeks and made lightning under the covers.

She's my big sister, but it always felt like I was the older one. She is short and pale-skinned, and I am tall and earth-stained. She is quiet and timid, and I am calculating and outraged. She has jet-black hair that could pull cargo ships to the bottom of the sea, but I don't think she knows that.

Her fists are small, but her eyes are big, and when you look into them you can't help but see a willow tree swaying in the wind. She is a rose petal and a thorn all in one, and when she pricks you, she draws blood.

All the times I was drinking, using drugs, wreaking havoc in the streets, she was next to me. Midnight tokes. Scrounging money to pay for the substances we needed. Hiding ourselves away during the day, binge-watching *Charmed*.

There was a time when we sat in a window, overlooking rows of tiny, colourful houses filled with people whose hands were wrinkled with a deep softness that only decades can shape. We passed a joint back and forth, vowing that if one of us were to die, the other would kill themselves. She was my Romeo and I was her Juliet as we put colourful pills on our tongues and sat on rooftops and cried together in a way that you can only cry with another person if you have seen the darkest parts of the world together.

"You wanna go do something reckless?" I asked her after inhaling a deep puff.

Her eyes glinted as she inhaled, her head nodding.

We fastened our robes, put slippers on our feet, and slid out the front door of the yellow duplex and into the crisp air of the night. We wandered up to the colourful, tiny homes, and in front of a red one stood dozens of lawn gnomes, proudly guarding the yard of whomever slumbered inside. We grabbed two of them and ran off, placing them in our basement and rolling around on the floor laughing.

"Do you think the woman who lives there will notice they're gone?" Orleane asked me.

"I have a feeling that someone who has that many must love them all equally." We shared a sinister chuckle.

Would they mourn the details of the things we took from them?

Would we mourn the details of all that was taken from us?

In the last semester of my master's degree at Columbia University, Orleane and I finally sat down, oceans apart, for our interview over the phone.

She told me about her earliest memory.

We were living in BC, sitting on the back deck at Grandma Shelly's, Frank's mom. Frank was about to get out of jail, serving time for another break and enter, and we sat there, eating kielbasa, awaiting his arrival. She remembers a tree in the backyard, and then finally, Frank, walking toward us, arms outstretched. I ran and gave him a big hug, but Orleane hung back, next to the tree, not wanting to approach. He waited expectantly, and then Mom ushered Orleane forward: "Give your dad a hug, Orleane." And so she left the protection of that tree, and hugged him.

"Do you remember when Mom told you that Frank wasn't your biological father?" I asked. "When did she tell you about Darcy?"

When we were living on the acreage, Orleane was about ten and Darcy was in the hospital, dying from complications of a drug overdose. Mom told her then, and asked Orleane if she wanted to see him. "I was just like, what the hell? I don't even know this person. 'Oh, by the way, this isn't your *real* dad. Your real dad's dying and he wants to meet ya!' Hahaha, no thanks!"

Like Chayla, Orleane was always afraid of Frank—from her earliest memories of him there was always fear.

"Did you ever tell Mom you felt that way about him?" I asked her.

"No, I didn't. I just pretended."

"You and Chayla both told me that you were always afraid of him. I wonder why he never scared me."

"I don't know. You're really just the person who tries to see the best in people. But also, maybe we did just have darker memories with him. Maybe he had a different relationship with you to fill that bond? I don't know. In the mind of a manipulator you never really know."

We talked about the happy memories, though Orleane doesn't recall many, but just like for Chayla and me, they were of the acreage. "It just felt like our own little world, running around outside, always getting into shit." I smiled as I let those memories steep.

After the happy memories, it was time to get into the harder ones. "Do you ever remember if we talked about what was happening to you? When he told me, everything was narrated through him. I don't think I ever actually asked you how you felt." I felt the hesitation in each word I spoke.

"No, we didn't. It was just like, it is what it is. I just thought, 'Okay, she knows. And if she knows, is this okay?' It made me start wondering and questioning. Looking back, I feel like he used that as a way to manipulate me. He told me, 'Oh, I told all these other people, and they're fine with it.' In actuality, he didn't tell them anything. But I believed it because he told you. He used that as a way to manipulate me even further. I was obviously getting older at that point, and wanted to live my own life. I started questioning things, and maybe he felt like he needed to get me back under his control."

Knowing that he used what he told me to further his agenda and justify his behaviour made me want to throw up on the grave I would happily dig for him. I had fantasized about his death for a long time, and that I would pull the trigger.

"When did you start questioning things?"

"Probably when I was fourteen. I forget what he was talking to me about one day, but afterward I was like, 'Oh, was that why you would sneak into my room in the middle of the night when I was nine years old?' He's like, 'You remember that?' 'Yeah.' I started making little jabs like that around fourteen years old. Even when he was doing one of his threats to go kill himself in the mountains, I was like, 'Well, why don't you just go do it?' He was *shocked* that I would say something like that."

I remembered those threats well. Anytime he was upset about something, he would scream, yell, drive recklessly, smash things, and then threaten to go shoot himself. I felt a small, insignificant surge of joy when Orleane told me what she said to him—her spirit fighting back. I let her words filter through my senses and thought back to all those years ago as if I was staring into a past that emanated a dull, sepia glow.

I could see the two of us, lying on the couch with our heads on opposite ends, legs intertwined, blankets on top, binge-watching MTV into the wee hours of the morning, snacks and weed crumbs littering the coffee table. Each time I would try to go to sleep, she would beg me to stay. Sometimes he would come out of his room, the one he made them share, asking if she was coming to bed, and we would say, "One more episode." Orleane always wanted to sleep next to me, and even after we were free of him, she was free of him, we still chose to sleep beside each other throughout the years, throughout the fights, throughout her pregnancy with Naia, until she gave birth—Naia then taking my place next to her. For twenty-one years, Orleane and I shared beds and rooms, friends and enemies, schemes and dreams, and drugs and bottles.

"I'll kill him for you, if you want me to," I told her one night when dawn was creeping up on us.

Tears welled in her eyes. "Living with himself is a better hell," she told me as the cherry from the cigarette we shared glowed.

"Did you ever think about telling me how you really felt?" I asked her.

"A couple of times I got really close to telling my friends Ashley and Sylvia. But something would stop me, and I just couldn't do it. I was just too afraid."

How do you even begin to speak the truth when that truth is a nightmare? The fear Frank instilled in me was enough to silence me for years. I can't even imagine the fear that she must have felt. What she had to endure. And the strength it took for her to finally tell our mom what was happening behind closed doors.

"How did you finally come to tell Mom?"

"I just needed to get the fuck out of there. It was horrible. I was just thinking, 'I can't... I can't keep this up. I can't have this baby.' And do you know what he told me when I said I wanted to get an abortion?"

My heart sank as I waited for her answer.

"He told me we would have to fly to BC because they don't do abortions in Edmonton."

"What the fuck!"

"Yeah! And I believed him!" She thought she was going to be forced to have the baby. Finally, she called Mom.

"The crazy thing about that too was that I got my cellphone wet and it wasn't working. I had it sitting in rice, waiting and waiting to see if it would work. I was in the bedroom and I think Frank was in the basement smoking crack. I remember thinking, 'I have to do it now, before he comes back up.' I didn't know when I would have another opportunity. By the grace of god, my phone turned on. I quickly called Mom and told her she needed to come get us. And she told me she was already on the way." Orleane then told Frank that Mom was coming to get us and we packed whatever we could. "I remember leaving and Frank was at the door. I don't know what they were saying to each other, but from the look on his face, he just knew. It was over. There was no hiding anymore."

"Why didn't he just come and take us?" I asked her.

"I can't remember exactly, but I remember telling him a reason why we had to go with Mom, something like, 'Oh, Mom wants us to live all together,' so he wouldn't get suspicious. I don't remember how long we were there for, but she eventually got all the evidence."

For days Orleane was lying in Mom's bed. She once picked up the notebook Mom left in the basket and tried to write in it, but she couldn't. She ripped out the paper and threw it away. She didn't know how to say the words—until Mom walked in the room, tears in her eyes, and told her, "My girl, I know ... and it's okay. I know."

"I just told her, 'Yes, it's true.' We both broke down crying and lay in her bed, crying together for about an hour." Relief washed over Orleane.

Then our mom booked the abortion and Orleane was stunned. "What? An abortion? We have to go to BC?" Mom told her, "No, here." It was then that Orleane realized another lie that Frank had fed her.

"That is so fucked." I shook my head, sickened that this man was my father.

I had to gulp down my heart before I could speak the words I needed an answer to. "Did you ever ... blame me?"

"No, not because you knew. We've been angry with each other, but I was never angry at you for that because I knew what a manipulator he was. Well, hold on, maybe, subconsciously I was angry at you, at all of you. Just because of the whole situation, though."

When I was dating the Man Who Taught Me How to Trust, my relationship with Orleane began unravelling. Not just a small fight here and there with us making up hours later, joints in hands. She had always been the sister guys loved, and I was always just the homie little sister who was one of the bros. When I was thirteen years old I wrote this poem:

My sister Orleane is every man's dream,
sometimes it makes me want to scream.
It's hard for her to comprehend,
but she's still my best friend.

One night, I brought Orleane over to C's house. The next morning, she told me that the Man Who Taught Me How to Trust told her she was the hotter sister. I immediately knew Orleane was lying, because this man did not talk like that. He was the epitome of a nice guy. I didn't know why Orleane was lying, but my gut felt it. The Man Who Taught Me How to Trust confirmed what my intuition already knew—that he would never say that. Why would my sister want to intentionally harm me? For the first time I thought maybe my sister was not someone I could trust to have my best interests at heart. Maybe she felt that I was being pulled closer to him and she wanted to keep me closer to her—I'm not sure.

When I asked her about this during our interview, she started crying. She didn't remember saying it, but she was crying because of the ways she used to intentionally hurt other people. I was used to being her punching bag because I was the closest person to her. I could take it and had been taking it, and after all, didn't I deserve it? I was the one who stayed silent while she was in pain for so many years. I felt it was my duty to be there for her, no matter how difficult it could be being close to her. I knew she didn't mean it. I knew she was a good person with a loving heart that had just been hurt, deeply. All I wanted was for her to be okay.

After I broke up with the Man Who Taught Me How to Trust, Orleane and I fell further apart. Orleane and I thrived when we partied together, perhaps because that's what we had always done, from far too young. I fell down that partying hole all summer after the breakup and Orleane and I always ended up in random apartments with mounds of cocaine on tables, in the back of clubs, and once, after a long night of bingeing, we even took a bath together and then cried about all we had endured in this life.

It never took me longer than a couple months to pull myself out of those drug and alcohol spirals, because I hated the lows and could only tolerate it for so long before I had to claw my way out. It took Orleane a while longer—how could it not?

Summer was over and it was time for me to go back to university, which meant I had to get my shit together again, but Orleane didn't have the same reason. She said that when I started university I thought I was better than everyone and that's why we grew apart, but deep down I didn't believe that for one second. I don't think she did, either. I thought I was better than drinking and doing drugs every weekend, but I knew she was better than that too. Every time Orleane drank I was her punching bag, carrying the brunt and weight of her verbal lashings. I started avoiding her.

One night, before I had a final exam first thing in the morning, my mom and Orleane went out drinking together and they were supposed to call me before 11 p.m. so I could give them a ride home. I told my mom if it was any later, they'd have to catch a cab. But later came and my phone was ringing off the hook until I answered at 2 a.m. They both berated me until I finally dragged myself out of my apartment. Orleane yelled at me the entire car ride home, telling me I was worthless, a selfish cunt, and not special. I vibrated with anger beside her, and honestly, if she wasn't the mother of my niece, who was waiting for her at home, I would have kicked her out on the highway right there.

One evening when I was at the gym, I got a text message from a random number telling me they knew my deepest darkest secret and if I didn't pay them $2,000, they would tell my whole family. The only people who knew my secret were my sisters and Alisha. I immediately messaged them, freaking out. I ended up in the bathroom dry heaving into the toilet. Not even an hour later, I got a text from Orleane saying, *It's me who sent that message, Chyana. I just wanted to remind you that you're not better than anyone else.*

My heart sank even lower. Why would my sister want to harm me? Why would she use my biggest shame to extort money out of me? I would never in a million years have thought it was her, but in that moment, I knew that I could no longer trust her. My eyes blurred as I ran to my car and sobbed behind the steering wheel.

We didn't make up until months later, when Mom forced us to come together on Christmas Eve. Orleane walked into my apartment, and there were no apologies between us, there never were—there was just her and a gift and us glossing over everything as if nothing had happened.

That's how it has always been between us. My love for her always overrides anything we have done to each other.

"Do you remember the last time you talked to him?" I asked her.

"In person it was the day we left. But there were a few times I was forced to speak with him over the phone, when Mom was getting evidence. Oh, actually, he did message me on Facebook a while back. I just remember feeling so angry and I told him, *Don't ever message me. I'll have a party on the day that you die.* It was so rude, hahaha. He was just saying all these Bible quotes. Like, I'm sorry, you can't change that fast, little buddy."

I wondered if there was a part of Orleane that ever loved or cared for him as a father.

"Fuck no! I despised him. He sickened me. I don't know how he had *everyone* fooled, but I saw him for who he was—this dark, lingering frickin' skinwalker. You know that one Halloween when he dressed up in that scary costume? With the long black wig, the black trench coat, and the scary makeup?"

I remembered the horror of that costume, how he loved dressing up as the scariest motherfucker—to the point that children were terrified to come up to our home.

"That's how I always saw him. From day fucking one."

PAHKOHTEW is when she dries by the fire, and I had to move close to it, feel the sweat from my skin evaporate and the heat from the flames warm each part of me, after traversing all the cycles of water. I think of the intergenerational trauma that has trickled into my life like the cycle of water.

Was I the groundwater?

Who was the cloud?

Who was the rain?

I want to be evaporation, condensation, but right now I am a Nehiyaw, a Cree, a Métis, and I also occupy white spaces in cities, away from mountains and trees. I was conceived and born in the Canadian Rockies and ran through canola fields in the plains and now my feet walk in a sea of brick buildings in New York City. Navigating a city is not much different from navigating the bush, just with different markers. None of this takes away who I am.

I am an Indian, a Native, an Aboriginal, an Indigenous. I can't keep up with the terms because they keep renegotiating who we are. What we deserve. Even my own people are bogged down with the politically correct way to introduce ourselves, and then we go on to persecute our kin who use the wrong term. That is a symptom of the colonized. It's exhausting. But I can also say that I am a smudger, a listening student, a dreamcatcher weaver, a drum maker, a girl in a Sweat, and a storyteller.

As much as I'm sad for that thirteen-year-old girl who once wrote that devastating letter to her father while he was in jail, I'm also incredibly proud of her. I found solace in filling the pages with words, and to this day, here I am, still finding solace on the page and making meaning of the world around me. That internal roadmap has led me here, reaching outward to continue to shape the woman that I am and still becoming. The woman who lives on with this trauma but breathes through it with strength and courage and the desire to make the next day better than the last, even when the next day is sometimes harder than the last.

Now I am a woman with tools and experience. Experience to know that the worst of the pain, the darkest of days are something that you can claw your way out of, one handful of dirt at a time, until eventually you have pushed and pulled your way out of your own grave.

Those of us who have done this, we emerge on the surface of the earth covered in dirt, skin more brown than ever before, but standing.

I can pinpoint three huge moments for me in terms of understanding myself and my history. The first was when I became a research assistant for the University of Alberta Prison Project. I thought back to when I sat on a metal seat in a cold booth facing a pane of Plexiglas. My father entered the cubicle on the other side of the barrier. He placed his veiny brown hand on the glass, and I brought mine up too, mirroring his. Nearly thirteen years later, this memory flashed before me as I was transcribing audio-recorded interviews with prisoners housed in Bowden Institution. Bowden is where my father was incarcerated for two and a half years for his crime.

How do you begin to forgive the unforgivable? Each day I listened to men tell their stories about what led to their incarcerations—my experience of intergenerational trauma coming full circle. More than 95 percent of inmates who were incarcerated for sexual abuse had also been abused physically and sexually as children. For the first time, I began to look at Frank not just as the Witigo in our lives, but as a person who was also once a small child. I had no idea when I was brought onto the project that it would allow me to heal parts of myself that hadn't been able to forgive Frank. Through listening to the horrors of the prisoners' childhoods, I reflected on the stories I had heard of the sexual and physical abuse Frank had endured.

Slowly, far away from him, outside of him, I forgave him, and it set me free.

The other two pivotal moments were studying trauma in fiction during my undergrad, and a class I took at Columbia called the Trauma Plot. In both of those classes, we studied psychoanalytic theory in conjunction with personal traumatic narratives, and I was given the tools, literature, and vocabulary to understand my own histories. Undergrad was where I first heard the term *intergenerational trauma.*

A therapist once told me that my trust issues would never get better and that was something I would have to live with. Fuck that guy, he was wrong.

I have a mind that is naturally inquisitive, seeking, and very direct, like a sponge for information. The only therapies that have actually helped me were somatic and EMDR, both using physical tactics to move through trauma and push it out of the body.

I am not healed because I have learned better coping techniques.

I am not healed because I have learned how to love myself—but I am continually healing each time I make a better decision for myself.

There is no such thing as healed—there is only movement along the spectrum of unawareness to awareness. Responses to events and emotions can become healthier, but it's possible that there will still be a feeling—a pit, a snag, or a small shadow internally that hints at an upset from before. Even if I can see and recognize how I am responding differently now, with that awareness there also comes the existence and acknowledgement of the way that I used to be—glimpses of the anxiously attached person who used to hold me hostage in situations and relationships that were either no longer for me or detrimental to my spiritual, physical, emotional, or mental well-being. If it wasn't "love" filling me up, it was drugs and drinking. I now live by the adage to never drink to feel better, only to feel even better.

Looking back was the only way to unravel the clues and become the woman who is here today. The one who wrote this book. The one who has confronted every dark corner of my psyche and every dark experience and forced a glimmer of light into them.

I went back to unravel.

I went back to make sense of the nonsensical.

I went back to lift the fog from my childhood Brothers Grimm fairy tale so that adult me learned how to love.

So that adult me learned how to trust.

So that adult me learned how to be in control of her life that had always been just out of her own wielding.

If I could reach backward enough to understand how something like this could happen to thousands and thousands of families, then perhaps this is my way of trying to ensure that it will never happen again, at least not in my lineage.

Perhaps it is my way of permeating my entire being with self-love, self-acceptance, self-appreciation, self-understanding so that I am a ready, strong, capable, and healthy partner for myself, and when the time comes that I finally meet someone I love enough to commit to, I will be ready for him too.

I held dear my magnifying glass as I examined the path I walked, and then followed it back further, until my fingers released the magnifying glass and it fell away—leaving it in the past because now I no longer need it to see up close. Now, I trust myself and my decisions. Now, I no longer have a use for my magnifying glass in my relationships because

I can choose whom to trust.

I can choose whom to trust.

I can choose whom to love.

My therapist says, "On a scale of one to ten, how truthful does that statement feel?"

It always felt like a lie.

After all this time, it feels true.

IF I AM A SNAKE, I'm not sure how many times I have undergone ecdysis, but this time feels different. When a snake prepares to shed its skin, it turns blue and its eyes become bone white, hindering its vision, before it rubs its head on something hard, abrasive—a rock or a tough piece of bark—tearing open the outer layer. It crawls through narrow passageways, allowing the fabric of its surroundings to grip on and slide the skin away from its body until the snake slips free from its old self. It is a solitary journey and must be left undisturbed, so as not to upset the process.

I dug, poked, and prodded so I could shed the last remaining dried-up skin off my brown body and make my way into the next chapter—no, the next book. But I want to keep the skin carcass, hold it delicately like a ribbon in my hands, look at its length and marvel at its delicacy and tenacity. I want to cradle this skin and offer it as a bow around my book, an offering to my Maries, all my ancestors who stood beside me this whole time.

Perhaps now I can place this book upon the bones, scoop the final pile of earth, and cover them softly.

I stand above the grave and remember the beginning—how I thought over and over about the entry into this story—our story of truth, or rather, the way that truth can be crafted.

I unravelled the lies to render our reality an honest one.

After all, we are an access point into a history—the grave consequence of schools and scoops for the Indigenous people of Turtle Island.

I wrote this story for all of us.

Who is the groundwater?
Who is the cloud?
Who is the rain?

Who are we all, if not dew?

Âsteyakamin

After a Big Wind and the Water Is Calm

I am Shel Silverstein
and Black Beauty
and Junie B. Jones as a young girl.
I am the one who fills the wagon
with grasses and carrots
and wildflowers
and walks it two kilometres
to feed the neighbour's horse
and brush the flies off her.
I am the one who named her Sparklingeyes.
I am one of those books
where you flip the pages really fast
and you see a creature morph
and evolve into something else.
I am Dr. Seuss.
Aren't we all?
I am mud pies in my mom's best pans
and dandelions plucked and weaved

and braided and placed on top of my head.
I am Biggie Smalls in the back of the Jimmy.
I am seven numbers or ten
pressed again and again.
A dial tone.
An incessant ring.
This mailbox is full.
I am laughter late at night
in hushed voices under the covers.
I am peeing myself
just because my sister dared me to.
I am sitting in a semi-dark room
at a table long and narrow and I am at the head.
I am all eyes on me
with old white faces staring at the dirty brown girl
with pinkened eyes.
None of them wonder why
or see the why
and I am just another brown girl
destined for a ditch along the highway.
Aren't I?
Aren't we all?
I am fifteen years old
and expelled from high school.
I am deemed sixteen in the court of law.
I am all my skipped classes
printed out on a piece of paper
that rests on the table
and an ounce of marijuana.

I'm done with this place anyways.
Aren't I?
I am eyes and a nose tucked away in books
and I am someone who strays—
but smart and scared enough
to know where is too far.
I am a failed attempt at suicide
and look how I shine in New York City
at Columbia University.
I am pride.
I am still sitting at long, narrow wooden tables
with white faces
but here my voice is heard.
Here, I am still a brown girl
but I am a brown girl who's going someplace good
and look if she can do it then you all can.
But I am not your example,
I am an exception.

Acknowledgements

THANK YOU TO the yellow duplex, for cradling us after we moved.

My mom, Orleane, Chayla—there isn't anyone else I would have chosen to walk this journey with. Hell and back, I'm grateful we were together.

Ling, as in sorry, as in you forgot your bling bling—from day one until the day we leave the physical realm, I will always be here for you and do whatever I can to help you in any moment you need it. You are my soulmate in the form of a sister and I would not have survived our childhood without you.

Delaney, as in rain, as in lemons, the woman you have grown into inspires me every single day and I am so blessed to have you as a best friend for the rest of my life.

Mr. Skoreyko, thank you for seeing me for who I really am.

Lorraine, you have been an angel on this earth for me.

Karyn Ball, trauma in fiction put me on this path.

Sandra Bucerius, you gave me so much healing through the prison project.

Justin, you gave me a space to start writing, and for that, you have a lifetime of my gratitude.

Julie Rak, you made me fall in love with memoir and stood beside me while I wrote the first words of this book.

Wendy Walters, Margo Jefferson, and Leslie Jamison—you three women pushed my writing beyond boundaries, made space for me, and inspired the best in me.

Sofia, our walks in Riverbank State Park brought me levity in the heavier moments of writing. Laughter and tears on couches. Your love, empathy, compassion, affection, and friendship continue to heal me every day.

Dea and Rikki, writing in Denmark surrounded by your love, humour, and warmth was the hearth I needed.

Claudia Cross, my agent—biscuits at Alice's Tea Cup with you changed my whole life.

Shirarose Wilensky, my editor, who saw the full scope of what I was aiming to achieve, and whose brilliance helped me get it there. Everyone at House of Anansi has been a divine gift.

Canada Council for the Arts allowed me freedom in writing this book.

My mother, again, because our hours-long phone calls multiple times a week, long walks deep in river valleys and mountains, matinees on Christmas Day, and your love and guidance made me into the woman I am today.

©Ava Noelle

CHYANA MARIE SAGE is a Cree, Métis, and Salish writer from Edmonton, Alberta. Her essay "Soar" won first place in the Edna Staebler Personal Essay Contest, then won Silver in the National Magazine Awards. She graduated with an MFA in creative non-fiction from Columbia University, where she taught as an adjunct professor. Her journalism has appeared in *HuffPost*, *The New Quarterly*, and the *Toronto Star*. She teaches Indigenous youth how to foster self-love and healing for Connected North and models in her spare time. When she isn't working, she is travelling and seeing nature around the world.